NOT JUST FOR THE POOR

Christian Perspectives on the Welfare State

*Report of the Social Policy Committee
of the Board for Social Responsibility*

CHURCH HOUSE PUBLISHING
Church House, Great Smith Street, London SW1P 3NZ

ISBN 0 7151 6570 4
GS 756

Published for the General Synod Board for Social Responsibility
by Church House Publishing

Printed in England by Edward Mortimer Ltd, Halifax and London

CONTENTS

iii

FOREWORD

The Kingdom of God involves making choices. It is about priorities. It is about deciding what we think is most important and taking decisive action in obedience to what we believe is true. Today we are confronted with some important choices concerning the future development of welfare provision in our society.

Two years ago, the Board for Social Responsibility published a consultative paper about the future of the welfare state. Many people responded and sent comments to us. We are very grateful for these contributions. They have provided the starting point for the work of the group which has produced this report.

This report endeavours to set before us the major principles which underlie the debate about the future direction for welfare services in our country. It seeks to provide us with a theological basis for a serious Christian contribution to this discussion. It presents us with the background of the present concern and with the essential facts and it outlines the main possibilities between which we have to choose.

I am most grateful to the group, ably assisted by Alison Webster, Margaret Jeffery and John Gladwin, for their hard and dedicated work in producing this important and readable report. They offer it as a contribution to enable the Church to consider the issues. The group itself represents a range of views on the subject. Whilst they as individuals reflect different opinions, they are united in presenting this report as a means of stimulating that response which I know it will receive.

Finally, this is a report about people — our brothers and sisters for whom Christ died. So we have begun with some human stories, and only after that gone on to look at the complex web of supporting structures that we call welfare.

September 1986   + Ronald Southwark
                    (Chairman, Social Policy Committee)

MEMBERS OF THE WORKING PARTY

Rev. Dr Michael Bayley (*in the Chair*)
Lecturer in Social Administration, Sheffield University

Robert Bessell
Managing Director, Retirement Security Ltd; formerly
Director, Warwickshire Social Services Department

Professor Ronald Preston
Professor Emeritus of Social and
Pastoral Theology, Manchester University

Malcolm Wicks
Director, Family Policy Studies Centre

Professor Paul Wilding
Professor of Social Administration, Manchester University

Board staff working with the group

Alison Webster (*Secretary to the Social Policy Committee and the working party*)
Margaret Jeffery
Prebendary John Gladwin

ACKNOWLEDGEMENTS

Many people have helped in the production of this report. We are grateful to all who commented on drafts and provided expert advice. In particular we would like to thank Professor Ford of the Department of Economics, Birmingham University, Professor Malcolm Johnson of the Open University, Canon Dr John Atherton of the William Temple Foundation and Professor John Pickering of the University of Manchester Institute of Science and Technology. They are not, however, responsible for the use we have made of the advice they gave. This report has only the authority of the Board by which it was prepared.

Shelter kindly allowed us to reproduce material from their magazine *Roof* for one of the case studies in Chapter 1. Figures 1, 2, 3 and Tables 1, 2, 3 are Crown copyright. They are reproduced with the permission of the Controller of Her Majesty's Stationery Office. We are grateful to *The Economist* for allowing us to use Table 2; to Penguin Books Ltd for Figure 4; to Richard Natkiel for Figure 5; and to Martin Robertson for the quotation in paragraph 4.19.

Chapter 1

INTRODUCTION AND CASE STUDIES

1.1   Shut your eyes and think of welfare. What comes into your mind? Tea and sympathy? The queue outside the DHSS? Your child benefit book? The ambulance speeding down the High Street? Or perhaps nothing very much? For 'welfare', after all, is not a word to make the blood race. It has a dry, old-fashioned ring to it, as if it is something that happens out there to other people.

1.2   Now put 'welfare' together with 'state', and what do you see? A system somewhere in a Town Hall? Something politicians argue about? Something useful but expensive? The images are probably even harder to summon, sliding off into slippery abstractions.

1.3   The aim of this report is to fill out the context of those two well-worn words. We hope that at least two things will be achieved. First, that readers will have a clearer idea of what is meant by 'the welfare state' and what the central issues for today are. Second, that they will be encouraged to think out what Christians and the Church can contribute to the debate, and if they are Christians, where they stand. Both steps are important, particularly in view of the next General Election, and the high place of welfare provision on the political agenda.

The Shape of the Report

1.4   What is the argument of this report? We begin with five people's experience of the welfare state. A middle-aged woman describes the welcome she and her husband gave to a mentally handicapped woman who had spent most of her life in a hospital. A man in his late sixties talks of his life looking after his frail mother. A young woman describes her sister's dying and death in a local hospice. A father tells of his life since being made redundant, and a woman recounts her experience of living in an unfit council flat.

1

1.5   These stories help our understanding of what the welfare state means in people's everyday lives. They are ordinary stories, not tales of the unexpected. They are a reminder that the welfare state is about 'us', not 'them'. Indeed it involves all of us with our unique and shared needs and responsibilities at various times in life.

1.6   The report goes on to examine aspects of Christian belief in relation to welfare issues. It is our hope that a faithful, theological process of reflection is at work throughout the report. Nevertheless it is in this section, especially, that some Christian tools for reflection and Christian values are examined. The particular importance of interdependence, a key theme of the report, is discussed.

1.7   The next four chapters set the scene. Chapter 3 describes the most important social trends that have affected Britain in the last 40 years and which will continue to have impact on welfare planning. Chapter 4 makes an assessment of the welfare state, paying as much attention to the enormous achievements and progress of the last 40 years as to the shortcomings and disappointments. Chapter 5 discusses the reasons for the breakdown of agreement about the philosophy of the welfare state and summarises four critical perspectives presented by feminists, the 'New Right', Marxists, and a group who emphasise the local and participatory nature of genuine welfare. Chapter 6 describes the ways in which welfare services are financed. All four chapters aim to give the reader background information necessary for an analysis of the key issues surrounding the welfare state.

1.8   The issues addressed in the final chapter are more controversial. Which features of present day society should Christians give thanks for and which should they criticise and oppose? What are the principles that are central when thinking about welfare provision for the future? What gets in the way of putting these principles into practice? And since there are a number of different options, which are the ways forward which seem both possible and creative?

Some Preliminary Points

A number of points need to be made at the outset.

CONSULTATION

1.9   This report differs from many church reports in two ways. First we have used a process of consultation. In March 1984 a brief discussion document was published.[1] Dioceses, church groups and individuals who were interested were given six months in which to comment. Some dioceses set up small groups to meet over a few weeks and discuss some of the issues. Other individuals read the document and sent in their own views. All the replies sprang from concern and direct experience. The responses were thoughtful and varied and have been immensely useful; the working party is grateful to all who took the trouble to write. Although it is impossible to do justice to the breadth and richness of the replies in the limited number of quotations included here, they have been a challenge to the working group, and a constant reminder of the audience and the readership. It also appears that the process was useful to those who wrote in. Several groups said they welcomed the challenge to clarify their ideas.

STORIES

1.10   The second way in which this report is different is in the use of case studies. As we remark of one of the critiques in Chapter 5, 'it alerts us to the truth that the ultimate test of the welfare state is what it means to people — not how it seems to professional staff, academics and politicians'. It is important therefore to include accounts of personal experience in an attempt to give readers a glimpse into other people's lives and what the welfare state means to them. If you have always had a steady income and a roof over your head and never had a day's serious illness in your life, it requires an effort and a leap of imagination to understand just what a difference the arrival of a home help at a convenient time or the Giro coming on the right day makes. Stories can help.

1.11   It is one of the positive developments of the last ten years that users of services have begun to be much more confident and assertive and ready to speak out. Despite the dangers of being anecdotal and obviously selective, their experience has its place in a report like this just as much as economic and social policy, biblical criticism and theological reflection.

OTHER SOURCES

1.12   An obvious source of evidence in this report has been the large amount of work already done on the objectives and

3

organisation of welfare services in this country. We write in the context of much detailed analysis of our present welfare state, carried out at all levels. For example, at national level the last two years have seen a major review of the social security system. This was announced by Norman Fowler, Secretary of State for Social Services, in spring 1984, and followed by Green and White Papers in 1985; new legislation was enacted in 1986.[2] The reforms proposed have provoked fierce debate and widespread public discussion; the process has undoubtedly been useful in raising public consciousness about social security. In the area of health, the Government has recently issued a Green Paper on primary health care.[3] The Swann report looked at educational achievement among ethnic minority groups.[4]

1.13   We also write in the context of several important initiatives in the voluntary sector. In housing policy a recent document is the *Report of the Inquiry into British Housing* chaired by the Duke of Edinburgh.[5] We also draw on the insights and recommendations of the report of the Archbishop's Commission on Urban Priority Areas, *Faith in the City.*[6] The implications of that report for personal attitudes and public policy in all parts of the country — not only the urban priority areas — are far-reaching.

1.14   A challenging contribution over the years has been made by groups like Church Action on Poverty, the Methodist Church's Mission alongside the Poor, and Church Action with the Unemployed. They have gone on asking questions about wealth and poverty and demanding that Christians find a faithful response. And there have been the stirring examples of the patient and skilful work carried out by Christians alongside people in all kinds of need.

LIMITS

1.15   Several of the groups who wrote to us urged us to be international in our approach. It is clear that the debate about how a late twentieth century society organises its welfare services cannot be undertaken in isolation. Britain shares significant social and economic trends with the whole of Western Europe. All these governments today must, for example, plan carefully for a larger elderly population, and for the effects of divorce. All of them face a shrinking manufacturing base, but increased productivity. The autonomy of each nation in decision-making is becoming less.

But to have included a European dimension would have enlarged the boundaries (and the length) of the report to an undesirable extent. So, apart from one or two places where comparative material seemed particularly useful, we have confined our discussion to the United Kingdom.

1.16   The same arguments apply to our decision not to include a world perspective. Christians do need to consider the well-being of Third World countries when thinking about priorities and about justice. But the question of power and poverty, trade and aid links between northern and southern hemispheres is a large and complex area, and we have not felt it right to enter it here. Other Board for Social Responsibility reports like *Transnational Corporations* and *Let Justice Flow* explore these questions.[7]

DEFINITIONS

1.17   Discussing the welfare state can feel like entering a semantic minefield. One of the characteristics of the present debate is the number of catch-phrases. Words and phrases like 'decentralisation', 'privatisation', 'targeting to need', 'universalism', 'back to Beveridge', 'community care', easily turn into slogans which raise the emotional blood pressure and prevent clear thinking. But they all denote crucially important approaches to organising services. They cannot be avoided if we are to look at the central issues facing policy makers today.

1.18   So it is not surprising that nearly all the people who wrote to us said how important it was to say clearly what is meant by 'the welfare state'. Out of many different definitions, there are two general approaches. One is to take a narrow view and concentrate on the core welfare services — social security, health, housing, social services, education. The other approach blurs the boundaries to include other public services (e.g. transport, police, employment and environmental services). It also points to the hidden forms of welfare, such as tax subsidies and occupational benefits which are not generally regarded as welfare but which contribute significantly to the well-being of those who benefit from them. We have chosen to operate principally with the former option, and put the main focus on the traditional core of services. But we also aim to show that welfare policy does not exist in isolation and is closely connected to fiscal, economic and employment policies.

5

LEAVING IT TO THE EXPERTS

1.19 This report is partly about poverty and those on very low incomes. It is also, however, about all of us whatever our income, and about the ways in which we all at different stages of our lives need practical and emotional help beyond that which may be able to be provided by our close kin. Debates about the welfare state, particularly those that have to do with costing and funding are complicated and daunting. But leaving it to the experts is dangerous. Each one of us is intimately and fundamentally affected by the quality of the services which we as a society organise for ourselves. Most of us care passionately about our children's health and schooling; most of us very much want to see our elderly relatives living happily with adequate support, and to know that that support will be there for us when we need it; most of us do mind if we see houses in our neighbourhood badly maintained. In that sense the welfare state is not just about the queue outside the DHSS Office. We are all experts and we all have something to say. The speaking out has begun in the form of Parent Teachers' Associations, patients' groups or claimants' unions. It is important that it continues.

THE CHRISTIAN RESPONSE

1.20 Three themes run through this report. One is interdependence. We argue that we need to live in a way which draws together dependence on God, confidence in ourselves as men and women, and care for each other. As one response put it 'We must all learn to give and receive, to retain our self-respect and respect others whatever our or their degree of dependency on family, friends, neighbour or statutory or voluntary social service.'[8]

1.21 A second theme concerns the small, the local and the personal. The big bureaucracies and systems of the late twentieth century cannot be avoided; they are vital. Pension schemes, for example, must be large to be viable. Bureaucracy should *not* be a dirty word. Indeed, we need to learn to value more highly the administrative and organisational skills which enable systems to serve the community efficiently and fairly. But the sheer scale of these institutions increases the danger of isolation, anonymity and remoteness. It is important that welfare services are able to respond to those aspects of the lives of individuals and neighbourhoods which are personal and intimate.

1.22   The third theme is about bringing to light hidden signs of hope. Some of the information in this report makes gloomy reading, but not all. To a surprising degree, given the current debates about our public services, there is much to celebrate. On many matters Christians will of course be undecided. There is nothing in the Bible which helps us determine whether, say, negative income tax or universal child benefit is a good idea or not. But the Bible does give us frameworks and important criteria. There are some firm principles on which Christians can agree and which will help us as we plan for the future. Above all, it is important that Christians listen to, and encourage, the voices which are creative. Then they will notice the signs of the kingdom of God.

Case Studies

1.23   The debate about the welfare state is often conducted in language of some detail and dryness, apparently far from the everyday experience which it fundamentally affects. So it is crucial not to banish that dimension of the discussion which is unashamedly down to earth. For this reason we hope that readers will keep people's names and faces before them, and will be mindful of the rich but complex ways in which life is lived in the late twentieth century. For this reason too we include here five accounts of day-to-day experience of the welfare state.

1. FROM HOSPITAL TO NEIGHBOURHOOD

1.24   Mrs Wright talks about Maureen, a mentally handicapped woman in her forties who has come to live with her.

> Sometimes I look at Maureen going off to the shops clutching my little grandson's hand and cannot believe that she spent 30 years in a mental handicap hospital. She has been living with me and my husband for a year now, and despite some ups and downs fits in really well.

> I suppose Maureen's story is like lots of people's in the days when there was little understanding of mental handicap. She was born just before the Second World War; when she was six months old she was abandoned in Central London by her mother, who had just discovered that Maureen had a mental handicap and would need special care all her life. The records aren't very clear, but she seems to have been sent to an orphanage for what they then called 'low grade

defectives', five years later to a special boarding school and then in her late teens to a large hospital outside London. My husband and I had been accepted on a local authority scheme to offer homes to adults needing a lot of care just at the point when nursing staff were wondering if Maureen could live a bit more independently.

Of course moving from the hospital to the spare room in our house was a very dramatic change for her and we had to take it very slowly. But it seems to have worked so far. How do we cope? Maureen has her DHSS money and we get a weekly allowance from the local authority. That covers clothing, heating, food, etc. Then she goes to an adult training centre every day where she does simple manual tasks; a minivan comes at 8.30 a.m. to pick her up, and brings her home at 4 p.m. At weekends a volunteer from a local befriending scheme visits and they go out together to the park or swimming pool. The local GP has all the hospital records, has got to know Maureen quite well, and we phone him right away if we are worried about anything. Occasionally one of the nurses from the hospital visits and brings photos of her old friends. I must say the other families on the estate were rather uncertain at first but they have now got used to Maureen's slow speech and partial hearing.

1.25 Maureen's move is the result of government policy to reduce the number of mentally ill and mentally handicapped adults living in long-stay hospitals. In her case the move has worked well. Mr and Mrs Wright get the support they need, and there are enough health and welfare resources in the area to enable care of her to be shared. There is no doubt that Maureen is learning skills and a new, though still limited, independence which she would not have achieved in hospital. This enrichment of her life would have been impossible without the planned provision of a range of public services — a small part of what we call the welfare state.

2. MOTHER AND SON
1.26 Mr Smith talks about life with his elderly mother.

I am 67 and retired from the Electricity Board a couple of years ago. Most of my life these days is taken up with looking after my old mother who is 93. Mum is still bright and cheerful but she is getting very frail as the months go by. I have to help her wash, get out of bed and dress; and I do get worried about leaving her alone. Sometimes even just nipping out to the shop for an extra pint of milk feels like a big risk.

You ask me if I get any help? Well, we live in a small village and are on good terms with most of our neighbours, although people do keep themselves to themselves. One of the neighbours has Mum over for tea every week; that's good, as I get some time for myself. Social Services help out too: one weekend a month Mum goes to an old people's home in Swindon 30 miles away. A bath attendant calls every week to give her a bath. But basically I'm on my own with her, and it's quite a struggle.

What is really worrying me now is that my mother is beginning to be incontinent and to forget what time of day or week it is. I'm beginning to suffer myself from arthritis and I get very tired with all the lifting and carrying. Sometimes I wonder what will happen to her if I can't go on any longer. And I must say I worry too about who will look after me when I am as old as she is.

1.27 Because of shortages, social services can often do little to help when the family is able to care. A case study such as this shows the cost of caring to the family, and gives a glimpse of what social services could do. Some home help, day care one or two days a week, for example, could make a big difference to Mrs Smith's — and her son's — well-being.

3. THE HOSPICE
1.28 A woman describes her sister's illness.

My sister Christine developed cancer in her mid-twenties. Quite quickly she had to give up work and undergo long periods of hospital treatment. We were all very shocked by Christine becoming ill like this: she'd always been so strong and healthy. Within six months she was unable to walk or really do very much for herself, and she died nine months after she first heard the news.

Looking back I think we all got a lot of help from the NHS. Christine was determined to know what was happening to her; the GP and the hospital doctors seemed to be open and honest and not out to pull the wool over anyone's eyes. We were always able to ring for advice or to discuss changes of medication. Through the NHS she got the best treatment available. We saw the service at its best and rejoiced at what we as taxpayers were helping to support.

I'm also glad that Christine was able to go into a hospice for her last few weeks. Her husband had been nursing her at home with help from the community nurse, GP, Social Services, family and friends. They were a great help but he was getting worn out by all the practical tasks and he had no energy left just to be with her quietly. The hospice staff were very good at discussing with Christine what she wanted

9

and at trying to control the pain without stopping her being herself. Somehow they seemed to have time for her as a person.

The staff knew that these last few weeks were really important for the whole family. They didn't pretend. They didn't try to take away our anger and sorrow and utter bewilderment at what was happening. This helped us live through those last weeks a bit more positively maybe, supporting each other, making the most of every precious minute, but also letting Christine be alone when she needed that.

4. LIVING FROM HAND TO MOUTH

1.29   Mr Taylor talks about life on social security.

We've never had much money, Mary and I, but we've always managed to make ends meet and turn out the kids properly. Then two years ago, the firm that I had worked for for fifteen years closed two of its factories. Sixty-five workers were laid off and I was one of them.

Of course there was redundancy money, and unemployment benefit for the first year. But now I'm on supplementary benefit which works out at £59.05 a week. We get the rent and child benefit for the two children on top, but with all the bills to pay there is never anything spare over at the end of the week. We dread the winter because of the fuel bills. And it's getting harder and harder to buy the bigger things, like shoes or winter anoraks for the children. We've given up all thought of a holiday, and are only just managing to pay for the TV and daily newspaper. Some weeks we can't even afford the basics.

Somehow, though, it's not only the cut in money coming in which has affected us as a family. It's hard to describe what it's like knowing that unless things change in this town I'll probably never get a job again. I'm 41 now, and there's a lot of life ahead of me. Of course I do mind not being able to go out for a drink with my friends like I did before. But it's more than that. Signing on at the dole office is a terrible experience. Some fortnights when I go down there I feel almost sorry for the staff: there are so many of us and so few of them, and the building is so grey and cold. But most of the time I feel angry with them for hassling us and not treating us as decent human beings. Anyone would think it was our fault for what's happened.

Last week I had to wait a couple of hours to sign on because they were short-staffed. Then the Giro didn't come through on the Friday from the DHSS office. Nothing came in the second post so I went out to the phone box at the other end of the estate. It took me half the afternoon to get through and then they told me they'd lost my papers.

What's ahead? Right now things look completely bleak. As I said, I can't see any chance of more work arriving in this town, and there's no way we could afford to move to another part of the country.

Mary's had a few casual part-time jobs but they only let us keep £4 of what she earns and the rest is knocked off our benefit. There's not much chance either of the children getting work here: only 30 out of 190 school leavers last year got permanent jobs. We're all beginning to get on each other's nerves, especially Mary and I. She's seeing the doctor at the moment and is on tranquillisers.

It would make a big difference if we had more money to live on. I'm not asking for riches — just enough to get by without counting every penny. But what I also want is proper treatment from the DHSS, and some understanding from other people about what unemployment is like. Right now it feels as if politicians in all the parties don't want to understand what it is like to have very little to live on, and basically don't care about what happens to us and our children. It makes me mad when the papers talk about 'dole scroungers' and conveniently forget to mention all the tax dodging by people who can afford accountants. I don't want charity or welfare: I want a job, a proper place to live, and some dignity.[9]

5. HOUSING STRESS

1.30   Some time ago, Pauline moved into her 20-year-old council flat. Within weeks of redecorating the family found black mould on their new paintwork. The kitchen, bathroom and bedrooms are now uninhabitable, their carpets so wet that the three children can't put toys on the floor, let alone sleep in the beds. Pauline started to be affected when she came out of hospital after an operation on her arm and could no longer do the essential task of wiping the mould off the walls.

I felt completely helpless. I started to do irrational things. My husband works some distance away but I was phoning him at work in the middle of the day and ordering him to come home to help me clean up. We had terrible rows. I'd scream at him, 'You don't care about me,' when it wasn't his fault at all.

At first I did nothing but cry and cry. I was in such a state that my husband was prepared to pack in the job he's been doing for years just so as to move house. I went to the doctor and asked him to write a letter for the housing department but he said, 'If I write one for you, they'll all want one.' He was right. Loads of my neighbours were going to him every day with terrible nerves.

The council hate the sight of me. I keep phoning and begging them to move me somewhere, anywhere, but of course they won't. One particularly bad day, I called them up and said I couldn't stand it any longer. I said I was leaving my husband and taking the kids with me because I couldn't bear to live in that place any more. They weren't interested. They said the problem was condensation and I was to leave my windows open. They thought I was just one more neurotic tenant. I was. I've lost two and a half stone over the first four months with worry.

I did a survey of 23 flats and found that 80 rooms were damp. I formed a tenants' association to fight the council, and every single tenant has joined. They're right behind me. They had a collection to pay my phone bill. We've been in the newspapers. We've demonstrated outside the council offices. And we're blowed if we're going to pay more rent in April if they don't do something to make our lives bearable.

1.31   Case studies reflect the experiences of individuals. Their strength is that they can help to bring alive what the provision of social services actually means to people. Maureen's life has been enriched by the policy of community care and the development of services to support her in the community. She could not live independently but she could live in semi-independence with support.

1.32   Mr Smith in our second case study, 'Mother and Son', valued highly the support he received in caring for his 93-year-old mother — but he needed more. The increasing number of very elderly people is a major moral challenge to our society. To maintain an acceptable quality of life for many such old people and their families, meals, home helps, meals on wheels, day care, sheltered housing are vital.

1.33   Suddenly, unpredictably, Christine needed enormously expensive medical care. In a few months she consumed medical care worth far more than her total lifetime earnings. What she needed could only be provided by some form of collective provision. Christine was also able to benefit from one of the most positive developments in modern medicine, the hospice. An attitude to caring for dying people which first found expression outside the NHS is beginning to have an impact on all hospitals in this country.

1.34   Mr Taylor, the father in our fourth case study 'Living from Hand to Mouth', was slowly and painfully adjusting to long-term unemployment. Social security payments meant that he and his family were kept from destitution and had a bare minimum of income for food, clothing, rent and fuel. But the process of claiming benefit was slow and complicated and often left Mr Taylor feeling devalued. Losing his job and becoming dependent on state benefits meant a loss of status and self-confidence affecting the whole family.

1.35   Housing plays an enormous part in people's well-being, as shown by our fifth case study. Pauline is not unusual in the problems she suffered. Tens of thousands of council properties built in the 1960s and 1970s have structural defects, have inadequate or expensive heating systems, and are subject to condensation. Design and layout may lead to insecurity, vandalism and crime. The sheer scale of many estates contributes to environmental and management problems.

1.36   These case studies show positive and negative aspects of services. There are other aspects we could have presented: the long waits in some hospitals for routine operations; the growing number of homeless families living in cramped bed and breakfast accommodation for months on end; mentally ill adults being put in prison because of inadequate resources in psychiatric hospitals. For every person like Maureen who has found a welcome in the community, there is likely to be another who has found only loneliness and inadequate support.

1.37   We have not attempted to present a complete picture through these stories. Our aim is simply to bring to life the importance of the welfare state to many people's lives. In very basic ways, how they live depends on what is provided.

1.38   There is, however, a major debate about how welfare services are provided, and what the role of the state should be in making such help available. Although there are no easy answers, it is vital that we equip ourselves with values and criteria that can help us judge which proposals for change are acceptable, and which are not. The next chapter considers some of the resources available through the Christian faith to assist us in making up our minds on these issues.

Chapter 2

WELFARE IN THE LIGHT OF CHRISTIAN BELIEF

It is surely the Church's role to make and debate statements of Christian belief, and to use these as the criteria against which Christians, at least, can judge social policy matters.[1]

2.1   This was one of a number of responses to the Board for Social Responsibility's consultative document which called for more theological work to be done. The responses not only looked for a full and clear statement of the theological and ethical perspectives underlying this issue, but they also wanted to see these perspectives influence the tone of the whole report.

> It is refreshing to see the paper begin with a serious look at the theological assumptions which are seen to be relevant. I would urge that this concern not be dropped after the introduction but woven into all subsequent discussion.[2]

2.2   There is a demand for a clear exposition of the theological themes which answer the question, 'Why is the Church tackling these issues?' Many feel that it is at the level of values that some of the most vital aspects of the debate about welfare are taking place. One Diocesan Social Responsibility Council went so far as to say:

> Even where there is a temptation to do otherwise because of the nature of the general debate, the Board for Social Responsibility should concentrate on values rather than resources.[3]

2.3   Many of the responses raised specific questions of values. They also included issues affecting resources, and problems of choice because resources are not unlimited. Matters such as justice, and distribution through the taxation system, the nature and form of the family, poverty and inequality, the relationship of corporate to individual responsibility, are raised in the responses which the Board for Social Responsibility received to its consultative document.

14

2.4   It is important to be clear about the relationship of the theological chapter to the rest of the report. The fact that it is in this chapter that we use the traditional resources of theology is not to be taken to mean that the rest of the report is not theological in character. There is a proper sense in which the whole report has a theological dimension to it. Christian thought on these matters requires a dialogue between theological criteria, a grasp of the nature of the present debate about welfare provision, insight into the dilemma of the choices we face and a willingness to hear the experience of the poor and disadvantaged in our society to whose needs services should be especially sensitive.

2.5   Within the Christian tradition, there have been many ways in which people have related their faith to the social order. Some have proved less than satisfactory. There is, however, a rich tradition of Christian social thought affecting welfare issues. Some of the most important recent work is referred to in the reading list at the end of this report. What we have sought to do in this chapter is to set out one approach which we believe does justice to what has stood the test of Christian experience. We believe it to be consistent with fundamental Christian beliefs.

The Creation of Human Life

2.6   The social character of our human life and the responsibilities and duties which attach to it are consistently and persistently set out in biblical thought and in the development of Christian belief. Human beings are made for each other. We can find our vocation in relationships with others, in the service of others, and in community with others. The ordering of society should give expression to these basic truths about what it means to be human. In Christian thought these matters have been understood as basic to the order of God's creation. The development of social organisations and institutions for the support of our life in society is not an accident of history. Without family, economic and political structures, there would be no social life. This is the sort of development to be expected of people who have been created in the image of God and who are called to exercise responsibility in the world which God made. So the question for Christians is not primarily concerned with whether we have an obligation to consider our life in the wider social

15

context but with how we do it. If we are to answer the question of how, we need to reflect on the framework of beliefs and values which we bring to the task as well as the nature of the situation we address.

2.7   Christian scripture and tradition assert that we humans share a common life and nature. This means not only that we have the same physical nature as a member of a species, but also that we have a common human nature with its glories and its weaknesses, sin and death. In theological terms all human beings are in solidarity with the first human beings and with each other.

2.8   This means two things in particular. First, it is the basis for the Christian stress on the unique worth of each individual person. We may not treat some as of more value than others. We have a duty to respect and enable each person's development and opportunity for personal growth and giving in service to others. Second, it is the basis for our sharing together in community, in a life of mutual service and obligation.

2.9   The creation theme stresses the diversity of human experience. The sharing of a common flesh and common nature is not meant to deny the diversity of human life and experience. This is emphasised in a number of ways. We share a common flesh, but we share it as male and female. Our sense of responsibility one for another, and the bonds of love to which we are called are formed between individuals, families and communities whose experience of being human is very different. Love does not equal 'sameness'; it is not simply a matter of fellow-feeling between people of like background and experience. It is the capacity to recognise, affirm and respond to the humanity God has given to the other person. Community — be it in marriage, family, or wider social groups — is made up of complementary experience, not of sameness of experience. The *koinonia* and unity of the Church is potentially enhanced rather than destroyed by the variety of gifts among its members (1 Cor. 12). Many have suggested that the New Testament picture of the body is the sign of what true human community is meant to be — a unity with a great diversity of parts and members. Human community is forged in the diversity of human life. It is in that context that we are to learn to practise shared responsibility and mutual care.

2.10   This picture of individuality finding its vocation, fulfilment and expression in community is, in Christian belief, a reflection of the character of God whose image is stamped on human life. We need, therefore, to seek for and develop social institutions which are consistent with this picture and which support and enable personal development within social relationships.

Interdependence in Human Life

2.11   There are a variety of ways in which we might explore the theme of interdependence as it relates to the debate about welfare provision. In the discussion paper which the Board for Social Responsibility produced to set this work in motion, interdependence was suggested as a crucial notion which made best sense of our faith in the context of the present debate about the welfare state. This clearly evoked a positive response.

> The crucial starting point, the basis of a specifically Christian understanding of 'social justice', 'social solidarity', the 'collectivist approach' to social welfare is surely, as the BSR report suggests, 'the interdependent quality of human life.'[4]

2.12   This report explores what the concept of interdependence means for us as individuals, as members of a society and as citizens with political obligations. All of us are in some measure dependent on others for our survival and fulfilment, and yet we all retain a degree of independence. We recognise that some people are reduced by the social order to a state of harmful dependence, and that their opportunities for personal development are excessively limited. It is these arguments about dependence and independence which lie at the heart of the current debate about the efficacy of the welfare state.

(a) IN OUR HUMAN EXPERIENCE
2.13   In the midst of this debate Christians, recalling the theme of creation, could find it helpful to stress the interdependent character of genuinely human social life. We have only to reflect on our own personal experience of growth and development in the family, in the economic context and as members of society, to realise the priority of the social dimension. Out of our proper dependence on others we discover our personal identity and

individuality. In turn this helps us lay the foundations for giving and receiving in our relationships to others. Our individuality thrives in the context of social experience. The Christian picture of a mature and balanced human life is about this sort of interdependence. This means that all of us need to have the opportunity and the means to give, and all of us must discover the liberty of being able to receive. That is bound, therefore, to lead us to question any form of relationship which is structured so that some are always potentially the givers and others always the receivers.

2.14   The simplicity of this conviction that human life is about giving and receiving is not meant to disguise the complexities of how this works out in practice. Christians have often used the language of giving and receiving to describe the expression of love in the relationships of women and men in marriage, of parents and children, of friends and families. The way the giving and receiving relationship is experienced changes as we pass through the different stages of our lives. It is important, however, to stress the reciprocal character of good relationships even in situations of dependence as with young children and their parents. Even very young children who rely on their parents for all basic care are nevertheless also contributors to the relationship.

2.15   The idea of interdependence opens the way for us to make a positive and creative use of the themes both of independence and dependence. Right at the heart of the Christian perspective on human life is the growth to maturity and responsible freedom of each individual person. There is a proper stress on individuality and independence. But there is also a clear acknowledgement that people must be open to receive from others. There is a proper stress on dependence and on the joys of receiving what others offer through their love and care.

(b) IN THE SOCIAL CONTEXT
2.16   Interdependence is not a denial either of independence or of dependence. It challenges any society which allows and encourages the independence of some at the expense of others, and which reinforces high levels of dependence and restricted responsibility for the poor, disadvantaged and vulnerable members of the society. What the notion of interdependence does

18

is to reinforce the moral obligation carried by the community as a whole for the well-being and liberty of each individual member. We are our sisters' and brothers' keeper! This is not to stifle their individuality but to provide the necessary framework for individuals to find and fulfil their vocations. We depend upon one another for the support needed to enable us to meet our obligations as citizens, as parents, as neighbours, for example. Independence and dependence are built into the experience of everyone in a society which acknowledges the interdependence of all its members. This means that no-one and no group is excluded from the corporate obligation, both to give and receive. If giving prevents receiving, or if receiving prevents giving, then healthy social relationships have been destroyed and questions must be asked about how and why this has happened. This is particularly relevant to the present debate about welfare. If the system has created and is creating dependence without opportunity, and is dividing the community into those who think they fend for themselves, and those whom they think of as 'scroungers' on the welfare state, it is fundamentally flawed when seen under the gaze of Christian values.

2.17   One of the unhealthy features of a society divided in this way is that it distorts people's view of each other. There is a strong tendency in such a disordered society for the strong to overestimate their capacity for good and to underestimate the capacity of dependent groups to accept greater freedom and responsibility for themselves. This requires the powerful to come to terms with the structural forces at work in society which inhibit the possibilities of others, less powerful than themselves, discovering and experiencing greater liberty and power over their own lives.

(c) IN THE OBLIGATIONS OF CITIZENSHIP
2.18   Understanding human life, made in the image of God, as involving interdependence in community has implications for the political sphere. Membership of society carries with it obligations. The rights and responsibilities of citizenship are affected by our understanding of mutuality in human life and experience. We depend one upon another. We carry obligations one for another. We must exercise our rights and duties as individual citizens in a manner consistent with our common life. In our responsibility

for the good government of society and for the provision of services which enable all to take their place in society as responsible members, we must be satisfied that we have given proper expression to that interdependence which is the hallmark of human life in its social setting.

2.19   The Christian tradition accepts the right of the authorities to collect taxes. The moral acceptability of the use of such public funds for the provision of services depends, in our context, on the answers given to two crucial questions. First, what sort of provision and support do people need for them to be able to affirm their membership of our own society? Second, what is required of our society and its citizens to ensure that such provision is made? If such provision requires at least some public services, there is a moral obligation on society to see that such provision is made. Such provision cannot be ruled out of order on moral grounds by describing it as 'coercive charity'. It is part of the obligation of interdependence. The social settings for people whether they are the family, the neighbourhood, or the wider political community are not accidental. These are the contexts in which we should expect people to live and grow, in which they have rights and for which they have obligations.

(d) IN THE PRESENT DEBATE
2.20   Much of the current debate about welfare is not about interdependence but can be made to contribute to the development of it. First there is concern about wrong kinds of dependence. One of the experiences of the past, and fears in the present, is that the lack of the provision of universally available services will lead increasingly to the poor and disadvantaged being made dependent on the 'charity' of the rich and advantaged. That sort of degrading and sub-human dependence was one of the experiences which the development of the welfare state was meant to destroy. In the past, much of the well-intentioned help given to the poor kept them in their place, and trapped them in poverty and reliance on personal charity. In a different way the present provision of public services by the state is sometimes accused of creating and reinforcing such dependence. The problem of poverty in our society has been persistent in spite of the development of welfare services. Instead of rescuing people from poverty, it is argued, the inadequacy and inflexibility of some state

provision has made people unhealthily dependent upon it. They are inhibited from acquiring the necessary resources to contribute to society. The reciprocity implicit in an understanding of human life as interdependent is prevented. Welfare provision, with these defects, instead of working to undermine such experience of wrongful dependence merely reinforces it. The opportunity for justice to be done so that everyone can share in responsibility and power is lost.

2.21   Second, some people emphasise the importance of each person's right to freedom to exercise responsibility as he or she chooses. Much of the philosophy associated with the 'New Right' makes play of such notions. Stress is placed on liberty for the individual and freedom as the key to social health. For example, both Nozick and Hayek have attacked the notion of the welfare state on this general ground.[5] However, an over-emphasis on independence at the expense of a proper acknowledgement of the social bonds and duties in human life can lead to the poorer and more vulnerable members of the community being inadequately supported and not offered any serious opportunity of escape from the poverty trap. It becomes independence for some and dependence for others.

2.22   The cynic might be tempted to comment that whichever way round the debate goes, the poor are always the losers. In a tightly ordered society they can become over-reliant on the state and be threatened with the loss of freedom. An open, free-market, competitive society constantly prevents the poor from participating through the exercise of choice and responsibility. If we are to make good and healthy progress through the notion of interdependence we have to develop policies which enable individuals, churches and neighbourhoods to assume responsibility for those tasks which can be best done by them.

The Biblical Concern for Justice and for the Poor

2.23   These themes associated with interdependence underlie a good deal of the biblical teaching on the poor. They are of particular relevance to our consideration of the welfare state especially as it relates to contemporary poverty in the United Kingdom. We need, therefore, to take careful account of the biblical tradition in this debate. The Old Testament law makes

21

specific provision for meeting the needs of the poor. There is both a recognition of the persistence of poverty in statements like 'the poor will never cease out of the land' (Deut. 15.11) and a refusal to accept the inevitability of poverty, as in 'there shall be no poor among you' (v.4). The provision for loans to the poor and for the Sabbath-year release of the poor from their debts is aimed at preventing people falling into permanent poverty. The radical provisions of the Law of Jubilee (Lev. 25.8ff) take this a stage further in providing for the restoration of lands to families who, in the intervening years, had been forced to sell up because of the pressures of poverty. Land could not be sold in perpetuity. Thus the law sought to prevent the creation of a society divided permanently between those who had been able to accumulate land and wealth and those forced into landless dependence upon them. There is no evidence to suggest that the Law of Jubilee was ever practised. Its presence in the law, however, is witness to the meaning of justice for the social order of Israel.

2.24   This concern for the poor is one of the obligations of the covenant. It is a consequence of the experience of Israel as a people who had been rescued from slavery and liberated for God's service. People who had experienced slavery, oppression and injustice and who had been redeemed by a God of justice and mercy, were to practise justice and mercy in all their personal and social relationships.

2.25   The prophets continued to press the social obligations of the covenant and its law upon the people of God. They denounced the manifest injustices of their time. The oppression of the poor and the injustices practised at many levels were seen by the prophets as the fruit of the religious and moral corruption and disobedience of the people. They 'trample upon the poor and take from him exactions of wheat' (Amos 5.10). They 'afflict the righteous', take bribes and 'turn aside the needy in the gate' (5.12). The wealthy live in luxury and plenty whilst the needy are abandoned. Religious and moral corruption go hand in hand. Isaiah calls the people to 'seek justice, correct oppression, defend the fatherless, plead for the widow' (Isaiah 1.17). He attacks the elders and leaders of the people:

> 'It is you who have devoured the vineyards. The spoil of the poor is in your houses. What do you mean by crushing my people, by grinding the face of the poor?' says the Lord God of Hosts (3.14,15).

2.26 Isaiah attacks the greed of the wealthy, their self-indulgence, intemperance, materialism and perversion of justice (5.8–23). He attacks those who corrupt the legal system to pervert justice, denying both the poor and widows their rights. The rights of the poor and needy built into the law of God are being denied by those who rule the people (10.1f). The righteousness of God is to find its response in righteous behaviour among his people, and that means justice for the poor in accordance with the divine law.

2.27 Jeremiah attacks the rich for their selfish accumulation of wealth through the exploitation of the poor (Jeremiah 22.13-16). He goes as far as to proclaim that the knowledge of the Lord was to be equated with the proper judgement of the cause of the poor and needy. The people could not be allowed to get away with the idea that they could be loyal servants of God while they encouraged injustice and took advantage of their power to oppress the poor. The indestructible link between religion, faith, and social obligation is clearly demonstrated by the Old Testament prophets.

2.28 The Wisdom literature in the Old Testament is more concerned with the attitudes and behaviour of individuals. How does a wise person conduct himself or herself in daily life? There are a number of places where the law and the words of the prophets concerning social obligation and organisation break through this more individual approach. The commonalty of the rich and the poor is stressed, as in 'The Lord is creator of them all' (Prov. 22.2 and 29.13). Those who dishonour the poor, therefore, dishonour their maker. This is the basis of the duty the powerful have towards the poor. The oppressive ruler of the poor is:

> like a driving rain that leaves no crops. It is justice that gives a nation stability. Corrupt rulers tear down peace and order (Prov. 29.4).

2.29 Although this teaching and these principles were primarily directed at Israel as the covenant people, the Old Testament acknowledges the universal rule of God to whom all peoples are accountable. The opening chapters of Amos are a particular example of the prophets pronouncing the judgement of God on the nations for their oppressive and brutal behaviour.

2.30 The early Christian Church accepted the Old Testament as Holy Scripture. The coming of Jesus and the establishment of the kingdom of God through his ministry represented the fulfilment of the promises of the law and prophets (but partly in paradoxical ways not seen in the Old Testament), not their abolition. Thus it is not surprising to find, in its own context, the early Church continuing to see compassionate response to the poor as an obligation on the faithful. Jesus himself witnessed to the nature of the kingdom in his own compassionate response to the needy and those rejected by the religious and political authorities of his time. The early Church was soon to find itself needing to make organised provision for the relief of the poor, for the care of widows and for the sick (Acts 6.1-6). St Paul, in encouraging the Corinthian Church to be generous in the collection for the Jerusalem Church, reminded his readers of the principles of faith supporting such action (2 Cor. Chapters 8,9). Furthermore, the early Church had begun to experience some of the temptations of wealth. A particular example of this is found in the epistle of James who warns against distinguishing in honour between the rich and the poor (James 2.1-9) and warns the rich who oppress the poor of their impending judgement by God (James 4.13-5.6). The themes of compassion and justice expressed in the Old Testament are incorporated into the New Testament.

2.31   What use can be made of this aspect of the biblical tradition? Our social situation is vastly different from that of the settings of the Old Testament or the early Church. This nation is not in a special covenant relationship to God. We are a pluralist society seeking to find practical ways of meeting the needs of all our citizens. We ought not to hide behind biblical models of practice in order to avoid the difficult task of devising structures for welfare provision which fit our own circumstances. The Bible is not meant to be used in that way. Its value is in the revelation it gives of the character and purpose of God, and what such understanding and experience of God does to our understanding of social life. The great themes of justice and compassion are of abiding importance. They are particularly relevant to the contemporary discussion about the provision of welfare.

Human Sin and Social Disintegration

2.32   Other important aspects of the biblical tradition such as understandings of sin and disintegration add further dimensions to our discussion. These themes take us forward to the Gospel and the meaning of the kingdom of God for our debate.

2.33   We live with the reality of injustice and a lack of love in the world. Good things are threatened with disintegration and corruption. The 'image of God' in human life is distorted, and so there is a tendency for the social order and human relationships to be abused, corrupted and undermined. Each person has been affected by sin. We see the evidence of this in the way in which individuals abuse good systems of provision to their own advantage, irrespective of the cost to others. Indeed, one of the key functions of law and social organisation is the protection of individuals from the abuses of others.

2.34   There is, however, a further complementary and corporate Christian perspective on the corrupting effect of sin. This further aspect is brought out in the work of Reinhold Niebuhr, who has had a profound and far-reaching effect on the development of Christian social thought in the twentieth century. In the light of his experience in Detroit of the corporate power of the motor industry, and its destructive effects on a community dependent on it, Reinhold Niebuhr developed a theological view of corporate life and institutions. *Moral Man and Immoral Society* is a statement of his conviction of the impossibility of directly approaching the problem of corporate power and structural sin with the Christian ethic of love.[6] That ethic may be appropriate at the level of close personal relationships. It does little on its own to deal with the large-scale problems of collective power. At this level the nearest the Christian ethic of love could approach the social issues was through the notion of justice. Niebuhr is one of the few who have faced the issue of collective power in terms of both private corporations and the power of government. He was able to use the Christian understanding of humanity in order to come to terms with the collective nature of our social experience. The transcendent love of God has to be mediated through a concern for justice in society.

2.35   All this suggests, at the very least, that we ought to be asking hard questions of all in this field from whatever perspective they approach the problems. On the one side it ought to be manifestly clear that in a fallen world, where vision is limited, we

25

ought not to throw the poor on the mercy of individual charity. The causes which people will support often have less to do with a genuine assessment of need than with what happens either to meet their desire to do something good or what appeals to the public mood of the time. The net result is an imbalance and inappropriateness of provision. There may be an unhealthy set of perceptions about the relationship between the giver and the receiver, and the creation of harmful dependence. That path has been tried and found wanting.

2.36   Against those who believe that the provision of massive public services is the answer to all need, it must be pointed out that we have enough experience of such provision to make us cautious about again creating excessive dependence and handing so much power over people's lives to public agencies without thinking through very carefully how such services can be accountable, sensitive and adaptable. If we think there is no escape from large and complex services we need to think much more about such questions of management and control. Neither should we underestimate the power of opinion to affect the balance of public services. Groups who carry few votes and whose needs are not greatly appealing, such as mentally handicapped people, single homeless people, confused elderly people, can find themselves at the bottom of the pile of priorities.

2.37   This leads us to note that organised provision and enforceable rights not only embody a vision of what is just and good, but also act as a structural barrier to hinder the effects of inequality and injustice in society and to resist the consequences of the destructive and selfish tendencies in the public mind and in individual attitudes. Where the weaker members of society possess rights they are protected against the vagaries of personal charity and the selfish restricted perspectives of the strong. An important aspect of the development of the welfare state was the concern to remove the fear of the threat of poverty, ill health and unemployment. If people propose to take this level of protection away from members of society at moments of need, then they have a duty to demonstrate that whatever replaces previous provision will offer at least the same, if not more, protection.

2.38   The task of assessing the adequacy of public institutions is a continuous one. The institutions of a welfare state are not exempt from the corrupting effects of sin. Like all corporate bodies they wield power and develop styles of life of their own. It is important to see therefore how they can be held to their purpose, to provide structures for justice in society. In the light of the Christian understanding of the fallenness of the world, we have both to resist idealistic notions about what individuals can achieve and to protect public services from corruption, insensitivity and lack of effective systems of accountability.

2.39   The poor are a living reminder to the rest of society of its fallibility and weakness. Extremes of wealth and poverty are a consequence of sin, and witness to the conscious or unconscious capacity for injustice of the rich and powerful, and the consequent disintegration of society. The way society responds to the poor is a crucial test of its moral health. We have already pointed to the consistency of such themes in the biblical record.

The Kingdom of God and Hope

2.40   The proclamation of the coming of the kingdom of God was central to the message of Jesus. By direct statement, by parable, and by unique action, Jesus proclaimed the coming of the kingdom into the world. 'The time has come, the kingdom of God is at hand, repent and believe the good news' is the record of Jesus' early proclamation in Mark's Gospel (1.14). The age of the kingdom is identified in the Gospels as the promised day of Jubilee as seen in Isaiah 61.1-2. The year of the Lord had come and there was 'good news for the poor, sight for the blind, liberty for the captive' (Luke 4.18-21).

2.41   The ministry of Jesus, as recorded in the Gospels, points to two aspects of the meaning of the kingdom of God for our life in the world. First, it concerns restoration. It is concerned with undoing and overcoming the corrupting effects of evil. In the ministry of Jesus we see individuals restored to health, to society, and to healthy human relationships. The kingdom of God is concerned with reaffirming and re-establishing the good order of creation. Second, it concerns transformation. The kingdom of God which Jesus brought into the world in his own person and ministry is more than restoration. In Jesus a new and final age dawned. The hopes and expectations expressed in the experience

27

of the old covenant find their fulfilment in Jesus. He is the promised Messiah who brings to the world the life of the new age of the rule of God. In Jesus we see the life of a transformed humanity in which the barriers between Jew and Gentile are undermined. Forgiveness is a liberating experience as stories like that of Zacchaeus show so dramatically. The transforming effect of the kingdom on him led to radical changes in his understanding and practice of tax collecting. A new understanding of love is set before the people — a love which embraces enemies and which goes the second mile. The ultimate transformation of the universe and of human experience is thus signalled in Jesus' ministry.

2.42 These truths have deep implications for the social experience of human living. The kingdom of God concerns new relationships in society between Jew and Gentile, governors and governed (Mark 10.45f), women and men, the included and the outcasts. The accepted orders are overturned in the life of God's kingdom. The last become the first and the first last. The kingdom of God concerns both new values and a new dynamic. It is both about love as freshly seen in Jesus and about the power of forgiveness offering the freedom to work for change.

2.43 The theme of the kingdom of God in the New Testament is taken much further. The story of the Gospel is not simply about the ministry of Jesus and our duty to imitate it in our own time and circumstances. Such a notion, on its own, might encourage rather optimistic notions of progress or drive the conscientious to despair. The radical nature of the meaning of the kingdom of God comes not only from the effect of Jesus' ministry but also and supremely from his death and resurrection. The life of the new age as Jesus revealed it in word and action led not to acceptance but to conflict. The establishment saw Jesus as a fundamental threat to its power and values. That challenge led to growing conflict and ultimately to the suffering and humiliation of Jesus on the cross. It appeared that the powers-that-be had obliterated the new way of the kingdom.

2.44 In the light of Jesus' resurrection and the Church's experience of new life, Christians came to see the crucifixion not just as a disaster but, in the purpose of God, as the moment of glory. Through the death of Jesus the kingdom of God was established beyond the capacity of the forces of evil to destroy it.

28

For Christians, therefore, the new age and the life of God's kingdom is experienced not through a steady progress of liberal development but out of conflict, suffering and pain.

2.45 Bringing this understanding of the kingdom of God alongside the structures (or kingdoms) of the world presents a radical challenge to society to face the powerful conflicts involved in embarking on new and more human possibilities in welfare provision. If the Church, therefore, is to be true to the meaning of God's kingdom it must speak clearly in word and deed about the interdependent nature of our social experience and its implication for all our relationships at both an individual and social level. It must also be ready to help its members and the wider community face up to conflict and, in the light of the central transforming experience of Christ crucified and risen, see the signs of hope which can accompany even the painful and difficult aspects of change. This may be the most important aspect of the Gospel which we need to live and proclaim in a deeply divided and fearful age.

2.46 The New Testament points us to the paradox of the kingdom of God. It is both a kingdom which has arrived in Jesus and is present, and also a kingdom whose full ultimate glory is yet to be realised. It is both 'now' and 'not yet'. Theology has always had to balance these two aspects of teaching about the kingdom. The dangers of stressing one to the exclusion of the other have always been present in the life of the Church. The stress on the presence and arrival of the kingdom, to the exclusion of the expectation of its full realisation still to come, may be used to bolster utopian expectations for our action now. The stress on the future coming of the kingdom may be used to bolster pessimistic notions of having to endure patiently the injustices of the present. The full Christian understanding will not permit either. We are both to seek ways of signalling the presence of God's kingdom here and now and to expect these to be open to change and development in new and different futures. The idealist who often espouses highly simplified blueprints for social issues, seeing these as the final and complete answer to the problems of injustice and poverty, needs to be reminded that the kingdom is yet to come. The pessimist who refuses to believe that it is possible to take any action to provide more just and effective solutions to present needs must be reminded that the kingdom of God has come and is present among us.

2.47 This paradox of the kingdom of God affects the way the Church is called to respond. It is important to remember that the kingdom of God is not to be identified with or restricted to the Church. The Church is called to bear witness to God's kingdom. It is to look for signs of its presence and to identify with them. The Church is to seek to order its own life, values and actions in the light of what it sees and understands of the kingdom of God as Jesus revealed it. There are both enduring realities and changing features in the way the Church bears witness to the meaning of the kingdom of God in matters such as welfare provision. The enduring realities are about commitment to the poor, a vision of human life reflecting the values of co-operation, interdependence and the dignity and sanctity of each particular person, and a concern for justice and compassion. The changing characteristics are about how these matters are given flesh in the social context of any age. For this we can receive help as we reflect on the struggle of the Church to respond to the challenges of the new society created by the development of industry. We have the heritage of generations of Christians who have sought to take action in the face of poverty, and to discover the social meaning of the Gospel in their own age. The imaginative thought of people such as William Temple and R. H. Tawney enabled a serious and pertinent Christian contribution to be made in the formative years of the modern welfare state. The paradox of the kingdom suggests that we ought not to be surprised that we are required to examine our own situation with the same imagination, in search of forms of provision which make good sense of the kingdom of God's enduring message of hope and transformation.

2.48 How are we to bear witness to these matters in the present debate about welfare provision? Clearly, Christians must continue to respond to the immediate needs of individuals and families in crisis through compassionate action on their behalf. Individual action, however, is not enough. The kingdom of God indicates a more comprehensive approach. The immediate problems of poverty, existing side by side with great wealth, are indicators of injustices in the social order. Christians need, therefore, to understand the root causes, to affirm healthy social values and to work for better corporate arrangements. Faithfulness to the insights of the kingdom of God takes us beyond charity to the need for radical change. The search for the kingdom, as both present and still to come, encourages us to seek for practical and attainable policies, to be imaginative in looking at new ideas and to be open to the future.

2.49   Thus the total shape of Christian believing — its conviction about creation and human life within it, its ability to understand and respond to the corruption of human life and society, and its experience of the kingdom as seen in Jesus' ministry and established in the mystery of his death and resurrection — provides the widest encouragement to our involvement in the social condition and challenge of our age. The particular challenge to the Church of how welfare services are to be provided in our society is one of the sharpest tests of its contemporary obedience.

Chapter 3

SOCIAL TRENDS

3.1 One of the tasks of this report is to discern ways of encouraging, creating and sustaining interdependence in the years to come. First, however, it is important to be equipped with information about what is happening in our society, what the changing needs are, and what are emerging as major challenges for central and local government, the voluntary sector, neighbourhoods, families and individuals. In this chapter we set out some of the most significant social trends: changes in the population, marriage and family patterns, the growth of Britain as a multiracial society, employment and unemployment, increasing poverty, and geographical inequality. We also point out what in our judgement these trends are likely to mean for welfare planning.

3.2 Choosing a timescale for such an exercise is necessarily somewhat arbitrary. The welfare state has its roots decades before the legislation of the 1940s and follows a tradition of centuries of organised poverty relief. But the decade of the 1940s is a convenient marker: What has happened to Britain since then? How do things look 40 years on? What does the future hold?

Population Changes

3.3 The population of the United Kingdom has grown steadily, increasing from 38.2 million in 1901 to 55.9 million in 1971. Since then the overall total has remained fairly level, with only slight growth expected for the years up to the end of the century. There are now just over 56 million people in the United Kingdom. But the relative proportions of children and elderly people have altered considerably, with a higher proportion of people aged 65 and over.[1]

3.4 One of the most important changes since the second world war, and indeed since the beginning of the century, is the rise in the number of elderly and very elderly people. This change is due largely to one of the great achievements of the twentieth century: the increasing life expectancy which improved sanitation, housing, nutrition and medical care have brought about. In 1981, for example, a new-born boy could expect to live to 70, and a girl to 76, whereas in 1901 their life expectancies were 48 and 52 respectively.[2] In 1901, one person in every twenty was aged over 65; by 1981 this figure was about one in every seven. While those aged 65 and over are expected to remain a more or less constant proportion of the total population until the end of the century, there is a significant ageing of the elderly population itself: among all pensioners the numbers aged 85 and over will increase by over 400,000 in Britain to over a million in 2001.[3] These changes can be seen in the following figure.

Figure 1 The elderly population: past, present and future

Source: Population projections by the Government Actuary. Mid-1983 based principal projections 1983-2023 OPCS PP2 no. 13.

3.5   Statistical evidence like this can lead to claims that the country is going to be faced with enormous 'burdens' of care and that the elderly people are 'problems' for our society. But, as Alan Walker points out, this is a dangerous 'demography of despair'.[4] Titmuss noted that 'Viewed historically it is difficult to understand why the gradual emergence in Britain of a more balanced age structure should be regarded as a "problem of ageing"'.[5] Living longer is something to be celebrated and valued. It is important to remember that improving standards of health and housing mean that most people aged between 65 and 74 will continue to lead active lives and need little extra help.[6] The number of elderly people in state-provided residential care remains small. At only 5 per cent of the total population of elderly people in 1981 it represents no significant increase since the turn of the century.[7]

IMPLICATIONS FOR WELFARE PLANNING
3.6   The ageing of the population is significant for welfare planning in several ways. It affects 'family life': more children will have grandparents and great-grandparents, and the potential for an extended family life will be increased. The relationships between work, support, care and income operate as a complex 'give and take' across generations. It is not a simple one-way process of adults assisting the very young and the very old. Many young families rely on older relatives for child care and this is particularly true for one-parent families.

3.7   However, the demographic trends also mean that more elderly people will need help and support. There will be greater calls on health and social services by very old people, and more call for suitable housing to meet their special needs. The assistance offered to elderly people in their homes, such as meals on wheels, and home helps, will need to increase if standards of provision are to be maintained. There will be budgetary implications. Elderly people make few demands on the adult education, prison and highway services. But they are heavy users of the health care and social security budgets.[8] A fuller discussion of this is found in Chapter 6.

3.8   At present the greater part of caring is done in the family. It is estimated that there are 1.3 million informal carers in the home — people acting as principal carers to adults and children with disabilities necessitating support with daily living. They have been termed the welfare state's 'forgotten army'.[9]

3.9   If community care in practice often means care by families, this in turn usually means care by women. Estimates vary, but the Equal Opportunities Commission found that 75 per cent of carers are women.[10, 11] For many women this means that their caring role through life will involve both responsibility for young children, and for one or more elderly relatives. Indeed, in many cases, looking after an elderly relative may become their major caring task — both in terms of the pressures and stresses involved, and in terms of the time spent daily, weekly and over the years. Welfare services will need to respond to this situation so that women are not trapped as family carers by social expectations and the lack of alternatives, and so that elderly people and people with disabilities do not find themselves forced to rely on family care when they themselves might prefer alternatives.

3.10   Other trends, too, put pressures on community care. For example, higher survival rates of children with severe disabilities and closure of some hospitals for mentally ill people are two of the developments that mean that more vulnerable people in the community need care and support.

Marriage and Patterns of Family Life

3.11 There is both continuity and change in marriage and family patterns. Despite all the talk of 'the breakdown of the family' and 'the family in crisis', the real picture is different. Marriage in Britain has never been more popular. This is perhaps a surprising statement — and it needs qualifying quickly — but as a broad historical generalisation it stands. Today it is likely that some nine out of ten men and women will marry at some time in their lives. Nine out of ten married couples will have children. Two in every three marriages are likely to be ended by death rather than divorce; eight out of ten people live in households headed by a married couple.[12]

3.12 Living together before marriage is certainly becoming more common. From the period 1979 to 1982 over 20 per cent of women marrying under the age of 35 had cohabited with their husbands before marriage, where the marriage was the first for both parties, and this was true of nearly 70 per cent of those women marrying where both parties had been married before. The corresponding percentages for women in the period 1970 to 1974 were 8 per cent and 42 per cent respectively. The incidence of cohabitation therefore has increased dramatically. But there is little evidence to suggest that cohabitation is replacing marriage and only 4 per cent of women aged 18 to 49 are cohabiting.[13] The usual pattern appears to be that the prospect of children leads to marriage but that a minority of couples form stable relationships and bring up children without marrying.

3.13   Another change is the increase in marriages ending in divorce. The divorce rate in England and Wales has risen six-fold in the last 20 years.[14] At current rates it can be estimated that one in three of first time marriages will end in divorce. The proportion at risk where one or both parties marry in their teens is very much higher. Half of those marriages involving a teenage woman will end in divorce, and three-fifths of those involving a teenage man.[15]

3.14   Family life today is further confused by both remarriage and redivorce. Currently just over one in three new marriages involves remarriage for one or both partners. Redivorce is on the increase, and the evidence suggests that second marriages are subject to greater stress and are more at risk of divorce than first ones.[16]

3.15   More children are affected by divorce. Indeed, some 60 per cent of divorcing couples have children under 16. If present trends continue one child in five will see his or her parents divorce before he or she reaches the age of 16. But again the continuities are important. Figure 2 shows that despite the trends described above, in 1982 of all children as many as 80 per cent were still living with both natural parents.

3.16   There has been a substantial increase in the number of one-parent families in recent years. Among the factors behind this are more divorces and more births outside marriage; it is also now less usual for children born outside marriage to be put forward for adoption. In many ways however the term 'one-parent family' is a misleading shorthand for a variety of situations: from that of a

Figure 2 Children under 18 by age
and where currently living,
Great Britain 1982

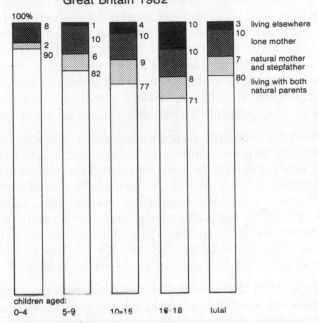

children aged:
0-4   5-9   10-15   16-18   total

Due to rounding, not all figures add up to 100%.
Source: GHS 1982 Table 4.31.

single unmarried mother of 19, to that of a widowed mother of 55, to that of a divorced father in his 40s. Most children have two living parents, although a significant minority are now living with just one of them. In 1971 an estimated 570,000 families in Great Britain were headed by just one parent. This number had grown to 750,000 by 1976 and it is now calculated that there are about a million one-parent families in the UK with the care of over 1.6 million children. About one in eight children therefore live for some of their childhood with just one parent.[17]

3.17 The number of one-parent families varies significantly from one part of the country to another. The highest proportion of one-parent families in Great Britain occurs in the inner London Boroughs. In 1981 33 per cent of all families with children in Lambeth were headed by one parent, followed by Hackney with 32 per cent.[18]

IMPLICATIONS FOR WELFARE PLANNING

3.18   In many respects these changing family patterns increase the demands on welfare services. The rise in the number of one-parent families leads to a greater demand for flexible child care; marriage breakdown and marital stress can lead to homelessness and the need for intervention by the local authority under the Homeless Persons legislation. The proper form of financial provision following divorce is still being debated, but at present family breakdown is likely to lead to a substantial reduction in income, and to considerable costs for the social security system.

3.19   Divorce necessarily affects children's relationships with their extended families. They tend to become cut off from one partner's family and have to learn to relate to a fresh set of people who are not blood relations. All concerned often need support and encouragement to develop new step-relationships successfully. One-parent families are particularly likely to need financial help and are more likely than two-parent families to be on low incomes. In 1984, the total average weekly income of one-parent families was less than half that of two-parent families.[19]

3.20   Policies will also need to take into account new patterns of living which are not the conventional nuclear family. As well as increased numbers of one-parent families and step-families, there are likely in the future to be more stable long-term homosexual and lesbian relationships, more single people caring for adult dependent relatives, and more adult mentally and physically handicapped people living alone in the community.

A Multiracial Society

3.21   A third important trend is the growth of Britain as a multiracial and multicultural nation. There have been minority ethnic groups living in Britain for centuries, mostly in London and some of the larger seaports. However the major arrivals of Commonwealth immigrants, first from the West Indies and later from the Indian subcontinent, took place during the late 1950s and 1960s. Primary immigration (i.e. of people other than dependants) from the New Commonwealth was significantly reduced by the 1962 Act, and was further restricted by legislation in 1965 and 1971. By 1982 New Commonwealth immigration had declined further and was almost entirely made up of dependants of people already settled here. In most years more people emigrate from Britain than arrive to settle, as has been the case for many generations.[20]

3.22 There is therefore an increasingly settled population of black groups in this country; at present about 4.2 per cent of the total. The Policy Studies Institute estimates that 40 per cent of the black population was born in Britain and more than half of those who are immigrants have lived here for more than 15 years. The largest groups are those of Caribbean, Indian, Pakistani and East African origin. But there are also significant numbers of people with Greek and Turkish Cypriot, Chinese and Bangladeshi origin.[21]

3.23 The position of black groups is receiving growing attention. There is clear evidence of the difficulties they encounter in this country and of the overt and hidden racism they face. Research into almost every aspect of life from housing allocation and employment, to representation in local and central government has shown the extent to which black people are at a disadvantage. They are more likely to experience poverty, overcrowding and poor quality housing.[22, 23]

3.24 This disadvantage has been recognised for some time by central Government. A 1975 White Paper made proposals to tackle racial discrimination, and stated 'The Government's proposals are based on a clear recognition of the proposition that the overwhelming majority of the coloured population is here to stay, that a substantial proportion of that population belongs to this country, and that the time has come for a determined effort by Government, by trade unions and by ordinary men and women, to ensure fair and equal treatment for all our people regardless of their race, colour and national origins. Racial discrimination and the remediable disadvantages experienced by sections of the community because of their colour or ethnic origins are not only morally unacceptable, not only individual injustices for which there must be remedies, but also a form of economic and social waste which we as a society cannot afford.'[24]

IMPLICATIONS FOR WELFARE PLANNING
3.25 Black workers have made a major contribution to many

branches of the welfare state, particularly in medical, nursing and in residential care for elderly people. But their contribution has not been balanced by an equal responsiveness to their needs nor by promotion. The evidence is that many black groups have found it difficult to make good use of the health and welfare services.[25] In some areas of welfare, notably the reception of children into care and admission to secure units, such as detention centres, a disproportionate number of black young people are involved. In other areas, such as the home help service, little has been done to adapt the service to black people's needs. They are seriously under-represented at senior levels of responsibility in the welfare services.

3.26 All the welfare services have important work to do in examining and monitoring their processes and procedures so that black people are not the victims either of bureaucratic policies ill-adapted to their special needs or of discriminatory policies.

3.27 A new, strong and settled black population challenges those involved in welfare provision to reconsider their assumptions and values. New services which are sensitive to the special needs and strengths of minority ethnic communities will continue to be necessary — for example offering interpreters to assist Asian women in ante-natal clinics, and the offering of a range of diet in elderly people's homes. Monitoring of services will continue to be necessary — for example to ensure that black people are not allocated inferior-standard housing and to attempt to improve the achievement record of young black people in schools. Perhaps most important of all, those responsible for recruitment and training will need to ensure that black people are not prevented from gaining promotion and making their contribution at a senior level.

Employment and Unemployment

3.28 There can be no doubting the fact that the British economy has experienced major change in the post-war years. One of the consequences has been that the manufacturing base of the British economy has shrunk considerably, and much of it has vanished. Employment in the manufacturing sector has fallen substantially, especially since 1979, and the vacuum created by the demise of manufacturing has not been filled.

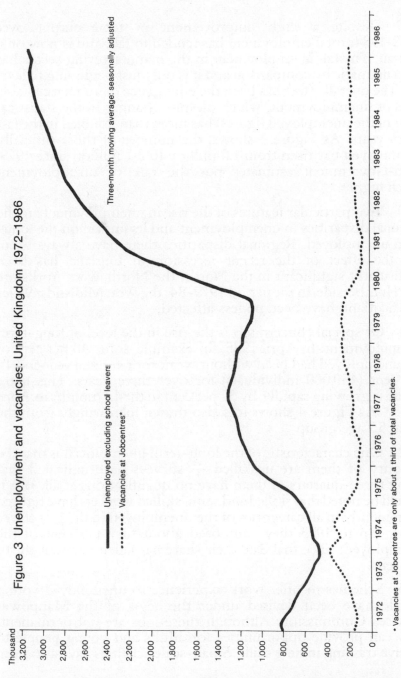

Figure 3 Unemployment and vacancies: United Kingdom 1972–1986

Three-month moving average: seasonally adjusted

—— Unemployed excluding school leavers

· · · · Vacancies at Jobcentres*

* Vacancies at Jobcentres are only about a third of total vacancies.

Source: *Employment Gazette* May 1986

3.29 Despite a slight improvement in total output over 1982-1984, total employment has tended to fall, and is now on a plateau. The fall in employment in the manufacturing sector has been dramatic by comparison and it is only just beginning to level off. The overall effect has been the emergence of an unacceptable level of unemployment, which (despite changes in the statistical basis of the unemployed figures) has more than doubled in the last seven years. As Figure 3 shows, the number of those officially unemployed has risen from 1.3 million to 3.1 million since 1979. Non-Government estimates put the rate of unemployment much higher.

3.30 Two particular features of the rise in unemployment are the regional disparities in unemployment and its impact on the long-term unemployed. Regional disparities there have always been; but the effect of the recent recession in England has been particularly significant in the North, the North West, Yorkshire and Humberside. In the period 1979-84, the West Midlands, Wales and Scotland have been no less affected.

3.31 Of special concern too is the rise in the level of long-term unemployment. In April 1985, for example, some 40 per cent of the unemployed had been without work for over one year and 14 per cent (450,000 individuals) for over three years. This latter group is growing rapidly, by 37 per cent in the 12 months to April 1985.[26] As Figure 4 shows it is also drawn increasingly from the 25 to 55 age group.

3.32 One characteristic of the long-term unemployed is that the majority of them are unskilled — surveys have indicated that about three-quarters of them have no qualifications at all. But it should be noted that skilled and semi-skilled workers have figured prominently in all categories of the unemployed in the past thirty years. Up to 1973 they composed about fifty per cent of the unemployed; since that date their share has fallen to about thirty per cent.

3.33 Schemes to offer work experience to unemployed young people have been devised under the aegis of the Manpower Services Commission. Although these jobs are not permanent, they can provide opportunities for adults and young people to receive training in new skills. Small-scale schemes have also been

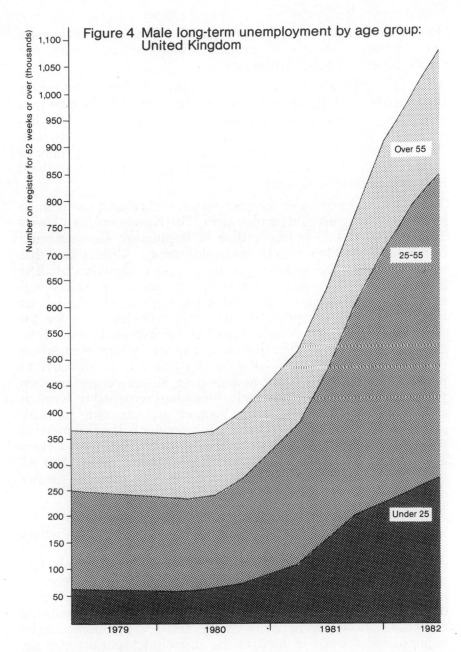

Figure 4 Male long-term unemployment by age group: United Kingdom

Source: Hawkins K. (1984)

developed to create new jobs through other government agencies and through successive projects designed to assist the establishment of small businesses.

3.34 It is difficult, however, to be optimistic about the means being used to handle long-term unemployment. Of the new jobs created in recent years a high proportion are part-time, and this has important implications for the structure of the labour market. Part-time work is often popular with women, enabling them to balance home and work commitments. But it can also trap them in low-paid dead-end work.

3.35 Another feature of the post-war years is that more women have been taking up paid employment. The *Women and Employment* Survey, undertaken by the Office of Population Censuses and Surveys and the Department of Employment in 1980, found that overall, women are spending an increasing proportion of their lives in paid employment. However, very few adopt the typical male pattern of continuous lifetime participation in the labour market. Most interruptions to women's working lives are for domestic reasons; it is common practice for women to work full-time until the birth of their first child. But a very high proportion of women return to work after having children, particularly to part-time work. This is not new — over 90 per cent of women whose first birth was in the early 1960s had returned to work at some stage. What is new is that women are returning to work more quickly after having a baby.[27] Today over half of all married women are in paid employment and two out of every five workers are women. The Board for Social Responsibility report *And All that is Unseen: Women and Work* looks at this topic in greater detail.[28]

3.36 While poverty is most often associated with the lack of a job, there is a significant number of full-time workers whose earnings are below the supplementary benefit level. In 1981, 260,000 families fell into this category.[29] But it is not only low pay which is a problem for these people. Low paid workers are highly vulnerable to unemployment, have access to fewer fringe benefits, and are more likely to experience poor working conditions. Low pay prevents saving, and few resources can be accumulated for use in hard times. Some intervention in wage setting has operated through equal pay legislation. Wages

Councils, until their abolition in 1985, set minimum wages rates for selected industries, holidays and holiday pay.

IMPLICATIONS FOR WELFARE PLANNING

3.37   Rising unemployment has serious implications for welfare services. Beveridge recognised this in his comment on unemployment in 1943, or what he called 'idleness'.

> Destruction of idleness means ensuring for every citizen a reasonable opportunity of productive service and of earning according to his service. It means maintenance of employment of labour and our other resources. Idleness is the largest and fiercest of the five giants and the most important to attack. If the giant Idleness can be destroyed, all the other aims of reconstruction come within reach. If not, they are out of reach in any serious sense and their formal achievement is futile.[30]

3.38   Unemployment underlies a wide range of other problems, particularly in inner cities. First there is the cost to the nation of supporting a large number of people on benefits, which will be more fully discussed in Chapter 6. Second, the effects of unemployment on individuals and their families and the communities in which they live are obvious enough. Many reports now exist documenting the impact of unemployment on health, educational aspirations, and of no less importance, on self-confidence and morale. All this serves to accentuate the more immediate effect of unemployment on living standards. The consequences for individuals and their families can be traumatic; and for those who are part of the long-term unemployed, there can seem to be no hope whatsoever of any improvement to their circumstances. They have neither the skills nor the education to rectify their position; and the longer they are unemployed, the less marketable are whatever skills they might have had.

3.39   As well as the serious effects of unemployment on welfare services, a number of other points relating to work and employment should be noted. Since a greater number of women with young children are now in part-time or full-time work there is an increased demand for child-care outside the home. Women's traditional availability for caring for elderly relatives is also reduced. The attempts to combat the effects of low pay are described in the next chapter.

Increasing Poverty

3.40   One consequence of the growing numbers of unemployed people and single parent households is the rise in the number of people living on social security benefits, and hence living on a very low income. One in eight of the population is now dependent on supplementary benefit as a primary source of income.[31]

3.41   The notion of poverty is notoriously difficult to define. Poverty of the kind which existed in the 1930s has been virtually abolished and overall standards of living have risen. But, given that state benefit levels are set at a low level (indeed even when rates were fixed after the second world war they were lower than Beveridge intended), a disturbingly large section of the population experiences considerable material hardship. The number of people living below, at or just over supplementary benefit level, has increased sharply recently.[32]

3.42   Levels of benefit have risen in real terms since they were first set after the second world war, but they remain very low when compared with average incomes. Under present regulations just £10.20 is allowed a week towards the basic expenses of caring for a child of ten years. Fuller discussion of the achievements and shortcomings of the social security system can be found in Chapter 4.

3.43   In this context it seems almost invidious to compare one group with another but the growing number of poor families is a particularly worrying social trend. Between 1979 and 1981 the number of families with children in poverty rose by 580,000 to 1,171,000, so that by 1981 nearly one in four families with children was in poverty or on the margins of poverty. A survey by the Child Poverty Action Group has shown that families who have to live for any length of time on supplementary benefit have great difficulty making ends meet.[33] The reason for this is not bad management; most people living on benefits shop with enormous thought. But, however carefully they budget, they are likely to be constantly anxious about whether they can manage until the next Giro arrives, as well as suffering from the social exclusion and sense of alienation which often accompanies long-term poverty.

IMPLICATIONS FOR WELFARE PLANNING

3.44   Of the many implications for welfare planning of

increasing poverty in this country, two need particular emphasis. First, the rise in the number of people living solely on benefits increases the demand on welfare services. It is well documented that very low income is one of the factors closely associated with poor health, marital breakdown and mental illness. Welfare agencies of all kinds are reporting a rise in referrals. Those agencies which specialise in financial help and welfare rights advice are having particular difficulties coping with the extra demands.[34] The pressures are likely to get greater, not less.

3.45 Second, as pressures increase, health and welfare agencies will need to be vigilant about the way that they offer help. It seems likely that in some areas of welfare provision, such as health, housing and education, a growing number of the better off and employed population will choose to buy what they need privately. The risk is that those who cannot pay for what they need will suffer: as has often been argued, services directed only at the poor can turn out to be poor services. It will therefore be important that welfare services are organised in ways which do not make the users of the services feel like second-class citizens.

Geographical Inequality

3.46 The effects of these social trends are not spread uniformly throughout the country. Some areas experience much greater disadvantage than others. A striking example of this is provided by the regional differences in unemployment. Northern Ireland has remained the worst affected region; its average unemployment rate in 1983 was just over 20 per cent, compared with a United Kingdom average of about 13 per cent. At the other end of the scale, the South East continued to have the lowest unemployment rate at just over 9 per cent.

3.47 Regional variations do not present the whole of the picture. Within regions, there are significant differences. In Scotland the unemployment rate in September 1985 ranged from 25.79 per cent in the area centred on Irvine to 5.7 per cent on the Shetland Isles.[35] There is also the example of health. This is affected by many factors such as stress, the quality of housing, education, pollution, employment or the lack of it. Within the West Midlands, the chances of any one person dying tomorrow are much higher in central Birmingham than in Rugby, for example.[36]

3.48 Finally there is inequality within towns and cities. The report of the Archbishop's Commission on Urban Priority Areas, *Faith in the City*, has described carefully the cluster of different forms of disadvantage affecting many of our inner cities and outer local authority estates. 'What are now called urban priority areas are districts of specially disadvantaged character. They are places which suffer from economic decline, physical decay, and social disintegration' (1.17), and 'The nature of the inequality which burdens the UPAs can be elaborated in many different ways. UPAs shelter disproportionate numbers of vulnerable people — the unemployed, the unskilled, the uneducated, the sick, the old and the disadvantaged minority ethnic groups. They are places which suffer conspicuously from low income, dependence on state benefits and social security, ill health, crime, family breakdown and homelessness. The sombre statistics of all these conditions provide the details of the map of inequality' (1.23).[37]

IMPLICATIONS FOR WELFARE PLANNING

3.49 Variations in employment rates, health, condition of housing stock, levels of income and wealth present fundamental challenges. Planners face the hard task of directing scarce resources to those areas where the need is greatest while also ensuring good standards throughout the country. But by far the most important challenges concern economic policy rather than social policy. The divisions are already profound. If in the future they are allowed to grow deeper, if the north and the south, the affluent suburbs and the inner cities feel more and more like different worlds in one small island, there will be little welfare planners can do to redress the balance.

3.50 In this chapter, we have explored the challenges for welfare provision presented by the major changes in our society over the last 40 years, which will continue to influence the planning of services. The next chapter describes more fully the welfare provision which is already available, and makes an assessment of its achievements and shortcomings.

Chapter 4

THE WELFARE STATE: ACHIEVEMENTS AND SHORTCOMINGS

4.1 This chapter seeks to evaluate the achievements of the welfare state. Some writers have couched such assessments in terms of whether the welfare state has resulted in the establishment of an acceptable social minimum, whether it has resulted in a more equal society, whether it has fostered greater social stability, or whether it has given people greater freedom and control over their own lives. This chapter does not set out to make such grand judgements. Rather it concentrates on assessing state welfare provision in two ways, first, by comparing briefly what we have now with the provision which existed before 1945, and second, by assessing how far the original aims of the post-war legislation have been fulfilled. As in other parts of this report, we have confined our attention to the core welfare services of social security, health, housing, the personal social services and education.

Social Security

4.2 During the second world war, much attention was paid to planning for a better society after victory had been achieved. The hardship experienced by many as a result of the economic recession of the 1930s was a vivid memory and people became determined that such conditions should not be allowed to recur. In particular, the war-time evacuation from the cities revealed to many the extent of the deprivation experienced by some British people. Unemployment, however, had not been the only cause of poverty. Social surveys conducted in the 1930s revealed the extent of poverty among elderly people, and families with large numbers of children.[1]

4.3 In 1941, a committee was convened under the chairmanship of William Beveridge to devise a scheme based on the principle of social insurance, to assist people to make provision for times when

49

employment was interrupted, or ceased. A rudimentary scheme of this kind had existed since 1911 when Lloyd George introduced National Health Insurance for the lower paid, and unemployment insurance, at first only for workers in selected industries but later for nearly everyone. There also existed limited provision for pensions from 1908. Beveridge proposed that employed people should pay contributions to a social insurance fund. Everyone would pay flat-rate contributions which would vary between broad social groupings such as the self-employed, employed and housewives, for example. In return for these, flat-rate benefits would be given, which would provide the minimum income needed for subsistence. (This minimum income consisted of allowances for food, clothing, fuel and light, rent and a small margin for 'inefficiency in purchasing'.) Contributions were to be determined actuarially so that the weekly amount would, over a working lifetime, fund the proposed retirement pension and finance the average expected incidence of sickness and unemployment. People would be entitled to claim benefits for unemployment and sickness, a pension on retirement, medical treatment and funeral expenses. Maternity benefits, provision for widowhood and separation, and qualification for a retirement pension would be secured for housewives by the contributions of their husbands. Cash payments for unemployment or disability would continue as long as the need lasted, without a means test. In order to lessen the risk to families, Beveridge proposed that family allowances funded out of general taxation should be introduced. By this it was hoped not only to ensure sufficient income for families at all times, but also to encourage the much needed raising of the birth rate by helping those people who wanted children to be able to support them. There would be no allowance for the first child while one parent was working.

4.4 Beveridge realised that special provisions would have to be made for his pension plans. It was agreed that there would need to be a transition period of 20 years so that people could make sufficient contributions to the insurance fund in order to pay for their pensions. During this time, special provision would have to be made for those who had achieved partial qualification to benefit, and pensions would be paid at a lower rate than the final 20 year value.

4.5 Beveridge also expected that unemployment rates in the future would not exceed 8½ per cent, while never falling below 3½ per cent. If people did become unemployed, it was not expected that they would be out of work for very long so unemployment payments would be a general charge on the Fund, a pooling of risks.

THE IMPLEMENTATION OF THE BEVERIDGE SCHEME

4.6 During the first years of its operation, the scheme worked well. Unemployment levels were lower than had been expected and there were significant savings in this area. This disguised the fact that spending on pensions had been much higher than Beveridge had estimated. It was not long, however, before the fundamental principles of the scheme were transgressed.

4.7 First, there was a movement away from the principle of everyone paying the same contribution in order to receive a flat-rate benefit. Rising standards of living in the late 1950s were matched by demands for increased benefit payments and the Government decided to levy insurance contributions at a rate necessary to match the outgoings from the Fund. The increases in the flat-rate contributions affected lower paid workers most adversely; so payments graduated according to income were introduced, with the promise of graduated pensions and benefits. Since 1975, contributions have been directly related to earnings for those in receipt of a weekly wage within certain limits. For 1985-86, those limits were set at £35.50 and £265. In 1978, a comprehensive state earnings-related pension scheme was introduced.

4.8 Second, the link between current payments to the insurance fund in return for future benefits was broken. The Labour Government of 1945 had based much of its social legislation on the principles set out by Beveridge but one decision, more than any other, was to undermine the scheme. The Government rejected the idea of a transitional period during which the insurance fund should be built up and stipulated that pensions would be paid immediately at the final full value. This meant that there were large and growing deficits from the increasing burden of pensions which had not been paid for in terms of accumulated contributions. People were no longer providing for their own pensions but they were instead supporting existing beneficiaries.

4.9   In order to provide for those people who would inevitably slip through the insurance net or who only had partial entitlement to benefits under the insurance scheme, Beveridge proposed a scheme for national assistance financed from general taxation. It was envisaged that the need for this would diminish as more and more people became entitled to insurance benefits. By 1950, however, one-quarter of all national insurance claimants were also receiving national assistance to bring their incomes up to subsistence level.[2] More people became eligible for national assistance as inflation eroded the value of insurance benefits. National assistance payments were increased in line with inflation, whereas insurance payments by definition could not be. Additionally, in setting the levels of insurance benefits, Beveridge failed to solve the problem of how to adjust them to take adequate account of housing costs which were highly variable between households and places. Recourse had to be made to national assistance in order to bring national insurance benefits up to a level where people could afford their rents and rates.

THE ACHIEVEMENTS OF THE SOCIAL SECURITY SCHEME
4.10   Beveridge's scheme was designed within a particular social framework. Changes in post-war society meant that the original design had to be modified and new benefits introduced. The special provisions for families in particular have been changed. The vulnerability to poverty of low-income families with several children had been recognised by Beveridge. He recommended that family allowances should be given to families with two or more children. These were paid for the first time in 1946 but at a lower level than that recommended by Beveridge. At the same time, families with children could claim a child tax allowance, thus reducing the amount of income tax to be paid. This was of no benefit to those whose incomes were too low to be taxed but favoured higher rate tax payers most. The value of both allowances failed to keep pace with rising prices and as tax thresholds were eroded in value relative to wages, many more low-paid workers became liable for income tax.[3] By the mid-1960s, poverty among families on low incomes was a growing cause for concern. Family Income Supplement was introduced in 1971. This is a cash allowance which is paid to families whose heads of household are in work. The amount depends on the number and ages of

dependent children. It is accompanied by entitlement to free medical treatment and free school meals. In 1988, it is proposed to replace Family Income Supplement by a Family Credit scheme, whereby the entitlement to free school meals, milk and vitamins is to be replaced by cash allowances. In 1975, child benefit replaced family allowances. It was extended to the first child and increased in value. Child tax allowances were phased out progressively.

4.11   New benefits have been introduced to cater for some of those people whose needs were not covered by the original scheme. For example, whereas Beveridge's scheme included those who became disabled through industrial accidents, no special provisions were made for people who were born with a disability which impaired their ability to work. Since 1975, they have been able to claim a non-contributory invalidity pension. Prior to this time, many disabled people had to rely on national assistance. Other benefits have also been introduced. Since 1979, anyone over the age of two who needs attention or supervision by day or night because of severe disablement has been able to claim an attendance allowance. Mobility allowances, payable to anyone between 5 and 65 who is unable or virtually unable to walk, have been available since 1976.

4.12   Beveridge made no special arrangements to meet the needs of one-parent families. In recent years there has been a significant increase in the numbers of such families, resulting predominantly from an increased rate of marriage breakdown. Single parents receive a small addition to child benefit, and for those in work there is an enhanced tax allowance.

4.13   The second, very important, achievement of the social security system is that benefits have improved in real terms since 1945. For example, whereas a retired couple received in 1951 a pension equivalent to 30.3 per cent of the average male manual earnings, this had risen to 36.7 per cent by 1983.[4] With the exception of the benefits for children, the purchasing power of most benefits has doubled since 1950.

4.14   Another change in the social security system since 1948 was the introduction in 1966 of earnings-related supplements payable in addition to basic unemployment and sick pay. These were introduced in recognition that people's financial commitments, say for house purchase, are likely to stand in direct relation to their incomes, and need to be maintained during times of unemployment and sickness. The earnings-related supplements were seen as a contribution to achieving this end. The 1966 Social Security Act stipulated that the amount of flat-rate benefits and earnings-related supplements should not exceed 85 per cent of the previous gross earnings from work. This arrangement remained in force until 1982, when earnings-related supplements were abolished, partly because it was feared that they acted as a disincentive to work and partly to reduce expenditure.

4.15   The greatest merit of the social security scheme devised by Beveridge is that it does assure people of some income during times of hardship, however inadequate that income may be. The scheme has been modified to take account of changing circumstances, new benefits have been introduced to remedy deficiencies and to meet new social needs. In addition, most benefits have maintained their value in relation to prices and incomes. Finally, Beveridge did establish the notion of benefit as a right. A great deal of the humiliation experienced in the 1930s, particularly by the imposition of stringent means tests, has been removed. Nevertheless, the social security system has not measured up to its original aims on other grounds.

THE SHORTCOMINGS OF SOCIAL SECURITY
4.16   First, it is known that not all people entitled to claim benefits do so. While it is not easy to estimate how many people do not receive the help to which they are entitled, various estimates have been made which show, for example, that over one-quarter of those eligible do not claim supplementary benefit.[5] People may not be aware that help is available to them, or they may be bewildered by the complicated claims procedures, or they may see claiming as degrading.

4.17   Second, the very existence of some means-tested benefits 'traps' people in poverty. An increase in pay may result in increases in tax and national insurance contributions and loss of various means-tested benefits such as free school meals or free dental treatment, and the withdrawal of housing benefit, for example. For couples with children, there is a range of gross earnings for which net income does not increase with additional earnings. A married couple with four children in 1985 with weekly earnings of £60 had a net income of £110 after the addition of benefits. If their earnings had risen from £60 to £135, their net spending power would have remained at £110 because of the withdrawal of benefits and the increase of income tax.[6]

4.18   The greatest contemporary challenge to the social security system is unemployment. Beveridge assumed that unemployment would be low and of short duration. He saw unemployment as waste since it increased expenditure on benefits and reduced the income necessary to bear these costs. He also recognised that his scheme would break down in times of prolonged unemployment. It was prone to the same weakness as the scheme brought in by Lloyd George in 1911, which had run out of funds in the recession of the 1920s. Recent increases in the social security budget can, for the most part, be attributed to increases in unemployment, and the increasing length of time for which people are unemployed. After being out of work for a year, a person has to move from unemployment benefit to supplementary benefit. There are two levels at which supplementary benefit is paid for adults. There is a lower rate for those who are expected to receive supplementary benefit for a short time only, and a higher rate for those dependent on it for a long time. So, for example, elderly claimants receive the higher rate immediately. Other people are placed on the short-term lower rate for twelve months initially. After this, some people such as single parents are paid at the higher rate of benefit, but people who are unemployed remain in receipt of the lower short-term rate. People who are out of work for a long time experience particular hardship. The difference between the long and short-term rates for a family of four with two adults and two children under ten is just over £12 a week.

4.19   Finally, there is serious doubt whether the social security system has eradicated want, which was Beveridge's aim. His subsistence allowance only covered basic expenditure on food, clothing, fuel and light and rent. There was no expectation that people would need additional income to maintain a standard of living which matched that of the majority in an affluent society. David Donnison, chairman of the former Supplementary Benefits Commission, expressed it thus: 'To keep out of poverty, people must have an income which enables them to participate in the life of the community. They must be able, for example, to keep themselves reasonably fed, and well enough dressed to maintain their self-respect and to attend interviews for jobs with confidence. Their homes must be reasonably warm; their children should not feel shamed by the quality of their clothing; the family must be able to visit relatives, and to give them something on their birthdays and at Christmas time; they must be able to read newspapers, and retain their television sets and their membership of trade unions and churches. And they must be able to live in a way which ensures, so far as possible, that public officials, doctors, teachers, landlords and others treat them with the courtesy due to every member of the community'.[7] Apart from this, there is growing evidence from a wide range of research, public and private, that benefits are insufficient even to permit subsistence in Beveridge's terms. It has been said that all supplementary benefit will provide is a rather boring diet for a good manager with no vices. Over seven million people (one in eight of the total population) are dependent on supplementary benefit,[8] the benefit of last resort, and three million people in Great Britain actually depend on incomes below the supplementary benefit level.[9]

4.20   Whatever measure is adopted for the definition of poverty, there are large numbers of people, some say as many as 25 per cent of the population, who live in an economically precarious position with little or no margin for saving. In 1981 28 per cent of the population had incomes below 140 per cent of the supplementary benefit level.[10] These people can be pushed into poverty by unexpected events such as a death in the family or illness requiring extra heating. While the social security system may maintain physical existence for many, insufficient income is provided to overcome the disadvantages attendant on poverty in terms of housing, health and education. These disadvantages interact and reinforce each other, and predispose the individual to remain poor.

Health

4.21   Beveridge saw his social security scheme as only one part of a wider social policy. He was concerned about the poverty which often accompanied illness and advocated the establishment of a National Health Service as being essential in reducing sickness. The National Health Service established in 1948 promised to do two things. First, it would 'promote the establishment in England and Wales of a comprehensive health service designed to secure improvement in the physical and mental health of the people of England and Wales and the prevention, diagnosis and treatment of illness, and for that purpose to secure the effective provision of services'. Second, it promised service free at the point of use.

A COMPREHENSIVE SERVICE?

4.22 Prior to 1948, health care provision was not comprehensive. The distribution of health services was very uneven. GPs were self-employed and could choose where they would work. National Health Insurance provided limited medical benefits for men below certain levels of income. For their wives and children there was no insurance cover. Hospitals were provided privately or charitably, sometimes for the exclusive use of certain groups. Some had developed from the Poor Law provisions, and were often attached to the workhouses, and run by the local authorities.

4.23 At present the country is divided between 14 Regional Health Authorities. Within this framework the National Health Service provides hospital and specialist services, family practitioner services which include doctors, dentists, opticians and chemists, and community health services which aim to care for people at home, particularly the elderly, thus minimising the need for hospitalisation. Questions of variations in the quality of health care remain in regard to different areas, patient groups and social classes. The National Health Service started with a very uneven distribution of hospitals and other services and this imbalance has persisted. For example, some of the largest best-equipped hospitals are in areas from which many people have moved away. It is also generally recognised that the GP service in areas of multiple deprivation and in rural areas is under strain. There has been an attempt to redistribute resources to meet need more appropriately but while inequalities have narrowed, they have not been eliminated.

4.24 Since 1948, the development of more elaborate and expensive medicine and the use of new technology has meant that explicit choices have to be made about priorities. Expenditure has to be distributed between competing programmes. What determines whether expensive treatment should be made available to a few people or inexpensive treatment to many? Who decides and on what grounds which patients should receive treatment and others not?

4.25 Emphasis was to be placed under the National Health Service on the prevention of disease. There are two kinds of preventive care. The first has to do with the maintenance of health and the second is concerned with the early detection of diseases before patients are aware of being ill. Beyond the bounds of the National Health Service, there are many public health measures which have been introduced to prevent disease. The regulation of the water supply, refuse collection, food and drink regulations provide but a few examples. Health education comes under the general heading of preventive care, and is concerned to make people aware of the benefits of balanced diets, exercise, and of limiting drinking and smoking. The early detection of disease is also very important. Screening programmes, such as the mass X-rays of the 1950s, are therefore significant. Free dental examinations and eye-tests are part of the preventive dimension of the National Health Service.

THE IMPOSITION OF CHARGES

4.26 The National Health Service was to be free of charge. Prior to 1948 most people had to pay for medical attention. Throughout the nineteenth century a variety of health insurance schemes had grown up through which limited medical care could be purchased in return for a small weekly contribution. A system of national health insurance was introduced by Lloyd George in 1911 and by 1930 this covered over three-quarters of employed men but only 40 per cent of the population in general, since dependants were not included in the scheme.

4.27 Beveridge firmly believed that access to the health service should not be impeded by financial costs. He proposed that the health service should for the most part be funded out of general taxation, with a contribution from national insurance, and should be free of charge to everyone. It was estimated that the annual cost to the Treasury would be £170 million during the first three years.

The actual cost during the first year of operation was £402 million.[11] This was largely explained by people being able for the first time to meet needs for glasses and dentures which had been neglected under the pre-war arrangements.

4.28   The first departure from the 1948 principle of free access came in 1951. Concern at the levels of expenditure led to the imposition of charges for prescriptions. This was followed by charges for dental treatment and ophthalmic services. Exemptions were given to people in receipt of national assistance, schoolchildren and expectant mothers.

4.29   Charges are still in force and there is a wide range of exemptions, but these are not uniform. For example, sufferers from prescribed illnesses such as epilepsy or diabetes which need constant medication are exempt but people with chronic neurological disease, cancer or psycho-depressive illnesses must pay, albeit at a reduced rate. Similarly people with long-term chronic invalidity or disablement do not automatically qualify, unless they are in receipt of supplementary benefit. There is provision, however, for people to purchase a 'season ticket' which will give entitlement to drugs at slightly reduced cost for a period of four months or one year.

AN ASSESSMENT OF THE NATIONAL HEALTH SERVICE

4.30   Marked health variations between social groups still exist. For example, the DHSS report *Inequalities in Health* published in 1980 showed that Social Classes IV and V, that is semi-skilled and unskilled manual workers and their families, experience the greatest health disadvantages. Differences exist from birth. For example, the risk of death during the first month of life for a child born into Social Class V is double that of a child born into Social Class I. Statistics on illness also show marked class differences. People from higher social classes also make better use of the health service, particularly preventive services such as antenatal care. For some people a visit to a GP may entail taking time off work with a consequent loss of earnings. The level of charges for dental treatment may deter those people who have low incomes just above the qualifying limit for a free service from seeking help. There are wide differences in the average length which people have to wait for a hospital bed according to the condition requiring treatment. Even for the same ailment, waiting times are highly variable between health authorities, depending on the size of the hospital, the age structure of the population and the facilities within the hospital. Differences in health status, however, cannot be solely attributed to differential access and usage of the health service. Housing, education, employment or the lack of it, the quality of diet, pollution, the use of alcohol and tobacco all affect the health of the individual for good or ill.

4.31 We have discussed some of the weaknesses of the National Health Service. While recognising that the demands on such a service are potentially infinite, and expand as new treatments are found, it must be said that the quality of the service and its use are not uniform either socially or geographically. But the great pool of untreated illness and disease revealed by social surveys of the 1930s has been substantially reduced. The character of General Practice, the place where most people make contact with the health services, has changed out of recognition. For most people, the existence of a National Health Service, which is predominantly free of charge, has both enhanced the quality and extended the length of their lives.

Housing

4.32 Although good housing is essential to many other aspects of personal welfare, no government has ever implemented a systematically planned strategy for housing like those relating to social security or health. Government involvement in housing has been hesitant and piecemeal. Where intervention in the housing market has taken place it has been designed to ensure an adequate supply of dwellings, rather than to provide accommodation directly, and to encourage better standards of housing.

THE SUPPLY OF HOUSING

4.33 Nevertheless, the supply of housing by the state has been seen as necessary on occasions, particularly after the second world war. The destruction and damage caused by bombing and the virtual suspension of housebuilding during the war resulted in an acute shortage of accommodation. Local authority building could be planned and controlled in a way private-sector building could not, and so the Labour Government of 1945 initiated a major programme of building council houses. Local authorities were given increased subsidies by central government, a practice first instituted in 1919. The public sector now accounts for just under one-third of all housing tenures.

4.34 The government fostered the growth of housing associations during the 1960s and 1970s, and most of the funding for this sector of housing provision has come from the government. Housing associations have traditionally provided accommodation for people with special needs such as ex-prisoners, handicapped people, elderly people and ex-psychiatric hospital patients. Since 1974, housing associations have been encouraged to provide rented accommodation for fair rents for people on low incomes.

4.35 Indirect government intervention in the supply of housing has been by helping people with their housing costs. Since the second world war, the supply of private accommodation for rent has declined dramatically, from 61 per cent of all tenures in 1947 to 9 per cent in 1983, as alternative forms of investment have given greater rates of return.[12] The legislation relating to the rented sector reflects an interesting oscillation between measures designed to encourage investment in this sector and measures designed to protect the interests of tenants. One of the most significant pieces of legislation was the 1965 Rent Act which introduced security of tenure for tenants living in unfurnished accommodation. Under the Act 'fair' rents were to be agreed between tenant and landlord. It was hoped that rent levels would be such as to encourage the landlord to keep the property in good repair and to protect tenants from the effects of scarcity. Nevertheless, it became increasingly clear that many tenants could not meet these new rents, and help in the form of a national rebate scheme became available for the first time under the 1972 Housing Finance Act. Tenants could claim means-tested rent allowances, which were replaced in 1982 by housing benefit. This benefit is an income related subsidy, and is not a general subsidy available to everybody in the tenure group.

4.36 Owner occupiers also receive help with their housing costs indirectly through the tax relief attracted by mortgage interest payments on loans up to £30,000. During the 1950s and 1960s, rising incomes allowed many people to buy their own homes, a trend encouraged by both Labour and Conservative administrations. The ownership of property was, until 1963, taxed according to the assumed rent which the property would attract if it was let. Rateable values were used as letting values. However in post-war years these became a fraction of the real rental values. Because most people are not outright owners of a property since they are dependent on a building society loan, it was felt to be unfair that such people should be taxed on the full rental value of their property; they should, therefore, be granted tax relief on the interest of their outstanding loans to offset charges. In 1963, Parliament repealed the levy of tax on the rented value of the property. Mortgage tax relief was continued in order to encourage owner occupation. In 1985/1986 it is estimated that the Treasury forfeited over £4,750 million in this way, over one-fifth of which was allocated to people with incomes in excess of £20,000.[13]

BETTER HOUSING STANDARDS
4.37   Successive governments have also been concerned with the quality of accommodation available to people. Local authorities in the inner cities, for example, were encouraged by the 1974 Housing Act to designate areas where poor housing combined with poor social conditions as Housing Action Areas. Special powers were given to local authorities to offer improvement grants, to enforce repairs and to acquire property by compulsory purchase. In 1982, generous improvement grants were made available to people living in dwellings built before 1919. The number of improvement grants made to private owners in Great Britain rose from 171,000 in 1982 to 337,000 in 1984.[14]

AN ASSESSMENT OF HOUSING POLICY
4.38   The question remains as to whether or not the measures which make up British housing policy have succeeded in providing a decent home for everyone. There is much to applaud. There has been massive clearance of slum housing and the development of much high quality public sector housing. People with particular needs such as the elderly and disabled have had special provision made for them in the development of sheltered housing. Many more people, over 60 per cent of all households, own their homes. While it is undeniable that much has been

achieved since 1945 to ensure that the majority of people are well housed, trends are becoming apparent which must give rise to grave concern. First, there is a shortage of housing. While it is true that there is a crude surplus of housing over the number of households, no allowance is made for houses in poor condition which are empty while they are awaiting repairs, or second homes. No account is taken of those people who currently share accommodation but who would prefer to form independent households. Shelter puts the national shortage of housing at 800,000.[15] This must be set against a background of declining public expenditure on housing. Between 1979/80 and 1984/85 there was a reduction of over 50 per cent, from £8,242 million to £3,079 million.[16]

4.39   An acute shortage of private rented accommodation is reflected in the growing numbers of people who are homeless. Local authorities are responsible for providing accommodation for families and people with special needs, but accommodation is not readily available; homeless families may be placed in bed and breakfast accommodation or short-life housing. The cost to local authorities in London of the use of bed and breakfast accommodation was estimated to be over £26 million in 1985/1986.[17] The number of homeless households in Great Britain rose to 94,000 in 1984, and this does not include single people not in special need and childless couples who are not eligible for help.[18]

4.40   Finally, one of the greatest problems facing British housing is the rate at which dwellings are falling into disrepair. The House Condition Survey of 1981 showed that over one-fifth of the housing stock needed repairs costing over £2,500 at 1980 prices. Elderly people, both owner-occupiers and tenants of commercial landlords, and poorer people in all sectors are most likely to live in poor conditions. Much post-war local authority construction, particularly that which employed industrial building methods, has led to dwellings becoming unfit after relatively short periods of useful life. Demolition has not been matched by replacement. Added to which, some housing design and estate layouts have engendered feelings of insecurity among tenants, and the incidence of vandalism and crime has been high.

4.41   In conclusion, housing threatens to be one of the major problems of the coming decade. While the majority of the population have good homes, an increasing number of people find that their accommodation, or absence of it, has become a growing source of despair.

Personal Social Services

4.42   Most people have a clear idea of what teachers, doctors and dentists do: after all they have direct experience to go on. The personal social services are much less familiar. There is a popular image, accurate or inaccurate, of the foster mother, home help, or social worker in a child-abuse case, but on the whole there is only the haziest public knowledge of what social services departments offer.

DEVELOPMENT

4.43   Although compared with the NHS only a small percentage of the population comes into direct contact with personal social services, social services departments have over a short space of time found themselves with wide responsibilities. The principle lying behind the provision of our personal social services is a simple one: that within the broad range of welfare services there should be the offer of help tailored to the needs of individuals, families and community groups.

4.44   The personal social services in their present form date from the recommendations of the Seebohm Report in 1968.[19] The Report proposed the setting-up of 'a new local authority department, providing a community-based and family-orientated service, which will be available to all'. The desire was that 'as far as possible a family or individual in need should be served by a single social worker'. The Committee hoped that a unified department would provide better services for those in need.

4.45   Following this report, local authorities established social services departments, which embraced the former children's and welfare departments and some of the tasks of health departments. They grew rapidly during the early 1970s, employing increasing numbers of staff and investing in new community resources. At the same time their legislative duties grew. Their responsibilities now include:

(a) child care under a range of children's legislation.

(b) the provision and regulation of residential accommodation for elderly and disabled people under the National Assistance Act 1948 and Registered Homes Act 1984.

(c) welfare services for elderly and disabled people, chronically sick people and those suffering from mental disorder and mental handicap under legislation such as the Chronically Sick and Disabled Persons Act (1970) and the Mental Health Acts.

In England and Wales these duties do not extend to those on probation and needing after-care; nor, since the implementation of the Housing (Homeless Persons) Act 1977, do they include direct responsibility for homeless families.

4.46 What does all this involve? It is not possible to list all the tasks carried out by social services departments. What they offer varies from one local authority to another, and according to need and local priority. Nevertheless, their work can be seen to fall under three broad headings — *fieldwork* (offering assistance to clients in their own homes), *day care* (running, for example, family centres, luncheon clubs, day centres for people with mental illness who attend during the day), and *residential care* (running establishments for elderly people, children and adults with multiple handicaps, young people needing short-term intensive help and assistance).

4.47 Their tasks involve employing a wide range of workers with different kinds of skills. We mention here a few of the best known. Home helps, in many ways the backbone of the departments, visit elderly and physically disabled people in their homes and take on crucial and basic tasks like cleaning, washing, shopping and collecting pensions. Occupational therapists assist people who have reduced mobility; they aim to increase skills and confidence, as well as supplying practical aids for the home.

4.48 Social workers, based in area offices, hospitals or residential and day centres, can offer counselling, practical and emotional help; they are also required to be involved when children and young people are at risk and to assess mentally ill people who may be at risk to themselves or others. Their work may also involve recruiting, assessing and supporting volunteers and co-workers, for example, child minders, foster parents and adopters. Community workers encourage and support the growth of groups and organisations within the community. Since 1974 hospital social workers have been included in the personnel of the social services departments. Residential homes offering care to elderly people, severely mentally and physically handicapped people, and to a decreasing extent, children in care, are important resources within social services departments. The Seebohm Report made little mention of residential care, but half of the social services departments' expenditure is devoted to people who cannot for one reason or another live independently.

ACHIEVEMENTS AND SHORTCOMINGS

4.49　The achievements of the personal social services rarely hit the headlines. Those who use their services are often very vulnerable, likely to be experiencing poverty and to have had their self-confidence damaged by illness, poverty, and bad housing. The success stories may be as dramatic in their own ways as the heart transplant, but they are nearly always hidden. Change is often measured in tiny steps. It may be the mother of a mentally handicapped child finally admitting to the pressure she is under and daring to entrust her child to a council nursery for two days a week; an elderly man deciding that despite pressure from his relatives he does not want or need to go into a home; a young man who has been in care all his life finding a job.

4.50　Yet there are visible achievements to which social services departments have contributed since the 1940s. A greatly expanded range of services is now offered by most local authorities. For example, day care for children, elderly people and other groups, aids and adaptations for the homes of people with disabilities, advice on welfare benefits, are all now available in most parts of the country. At the same time standards have risen, with more residential homes now employing trained staff.

4.51　There is also a greater understanding of the special needs of many groups, especially children in care. The creation and development of Children's Departments in post-war Britain made a real difference to the lives of many children in care. The Children

Act 1948 offered them, for the first time, the right to be treated as all other children. Although nearly 40 years later the experience of children in care is still a matter of concern,[20] the commitment to preventive work with families is still strong, as is the desire to find permanent family homes for children who are unable to live with their natural parents. There is still a need for some residential provision, mainly for older children, but the days when large children's homes were needed seem to be over. The fostering and adoption over the years of many 'hard to place' children with handicaps has been a particular achievement.

4.52   The last decades have seen, too, a growing awareness, much of it formalised in legislation, of the needs of people who are disabled, mentally ill and mentally handicapped. There are now many adults and children with mental or physical disabilities who can look forward to a fuller and more independent life than up to now. Some progress has been made in the translation of the ideals of 'care in the community' into practice, although the present level of resources in the community must raise doubts about the extent to which this enlightened policy can be carried out successfully.

4.53   As well as services increasing in numbers and more help being offered, there has been much imaginative and innovative work; for example, in the growth of schemes offering short-term care to elderly or disabled people. Some parts of the country have experimented with local offices serving a smaller population, and a few have combined with other local authority departments to give advice on housing and welfare rights.

4.54   But the failures and shortcomings of social services departments are also clear. They have not generally been good at communicating to the outside world what they do, and the result has been a mixed response of high expectations and suspicion. The Barclay Report of 1982, an enquiry into the role and tasks of social workers, comments in its opening paragraph: 'Too much is generally expected of social workers... They operate uneasily on the frontier between what appears to be almost limitless needs on the one hand and an inadequate pool of resources to meet those needs on the other'.[21] These expectations are highest in the field of child care. Every child abuse case where the local authority is involved, particularly those where the child dies, shows the tensions inherent in a system which attempts to offer both 'state care' and 'state policing', and where the workers involved have to weigh up the different rights of children and parents.

4.55   Resources are still inadequate. There are waiting lists for many facilities, fewer home helps than necessary and a form of hidden rationing has emerged. To quote again from the Barclay Report: 'We have slowed down the expansion of social services without necessarily accepting some of the implications. We may have as our aim a service available to all in need, but we expect it to be quietly rationed. We may wish to think that we have left the Poor Law behind us but fail to see the stigma and selectivity which for many are the practical realities of social services and social work. We talk in terms of client groups and thus disguise the relative poverty that unites almost all who seek social work assistance.'

4.56   The result is that there are still many people with a real need for assistance who cannot obtain it. The last five years have witnessed a greater awareness of the enormous needs of those caring long-term for elderly and disabled relatives. But many of them receive little or no help from the social services.

4.57   Another shortcoming shared with other services is the difficulty social services departments have in offering equal access to all the people in the communities they serve. It is not easy to ensure that black groups, who are often at a double disadvantage both from poverty and from racial discrimination, know about and have access to the help available. It has become evident that departments need to examine their own practices and policies in the light of a better understanding about the ways in which racism may be manifested covertly and unconsciously, both at the personal and institutional level. Particular instances are the growing debates about trans-racial adoption and fostering, and the practice of placing black children received into care with white families.

4.58   Overall, it must be said that social services departments have not been good at making it possible for those whom they serve and other members of society to participate in the services they are offering. They remain for the most part services done *to* people rather than *with* them.

Education

4.59   It was not until 1870 that the state undertook to provide a basic education for all children. Throughout the nineteenth century attitudes to universal education were equivocal. Early on, it was feared that any widening of horizons for working class children in particular would cause them to rebel against their circumstances. However with the progress of the Industrial Revolution and the increasing concentration of people in large urban areas, it was recognised that some education would be necessary in order to meet basic requirements for literacy among factory workers, and to prevent 'agitators' feeding on ignorance. Emphasis was laid on the teaching of morality and the inculcation of right attitudes. Particular encouragement was given to the founding of the Mechanics' Institutes and the voluntary education provided by the National Society and the British and Foreign Schools Society.

4.60   The principle of the 1944 Education Act was to provide each child with the type of education to which he or she was best fitted, regardless of income or social background. By this it was hoped to reduce the disparities based on social class and to promote social mobility. The system which emerged after the war provided primary schooling until the child reached 11, followed by secondary education up to 15 at least in any one of three kinds of school, namely grammar, technical or secondary modern. Part of the Act which was never implemented was the compulsory part-time education to 18 for those who left full-time education at 15.

4.61   Over the last 40 years there have been some significant changes to this framework. Concern grew during the 1950s about the lack of movement between the different types of school. Insufficient attention had been paid to technical education, and in some areas technical schools had not been set up. The opportunities for children in secondary modern schools were found to be restricted. The Labour Government of 1965 requested all local education authorities to devise plans for reorganising schools along comprehensive lines in order to break down the social segregation between the different types of school and to offer a wide range of opportunities to all children to acquire the education best fitted to their needs. By 1977 over four-fifths of children educated in the public sector attended comprehensive schools.[22] In 1973 the school leaving age was raised to 16 in the hope that children would acquire additional qualifications before seeking work.

ACHIEVEMENTS OF THE EDUCATION SYSTEM

4.62 All children in Britain are entitled to receive a basic education free of charge for 11 years. Over the last 40 years the content of the curriculum has changed significantly to encompass new subjects and skills. More people now leave school with some qualifications. In 1969, only 38 per cent of school leavers had 'O' or 'A' level passes. By 1983, more than 52 per cent had such qualifications. During the same period, the proportion of children leaving school with no qualifications fell from 50 per cent to 10 per cent.[23] There has been a determination to allow children to develop special talents in music and sport, for example through the provision of music centres and specialist peripatetic teachers. Children have been encouraged to participate in community activities. More recently there has been a concern to educate children for life in a multicultural society. The possibility of receiving further education has been extended, particularly to working class children, through the local authority grants system. Over two-fifths of all children aged three and four receive some education in nursery or primary schools.[24]

4.63 An education system is not confined to providing an academic education. Concern for physical fitness and the maintenance of the health of the child has been demonstrated in several ways. Compulsory physical education was introduced, and free milk was made available to supplement the child's diet. (This was removed in 1968 from secondary schools, and from junior schools in 1971.) All children have regular medical checks, and can be referred to educational psychologists if necessary. Additionally, most schools also provide courses in personal and social development, and offer health and sex education as part of the concern for the development of the whole person.

4.64 Special measures have been taken to ensure that in theory at least a child's education should not be undermined by the lack of parental income. Local education authorities may, at their discretion, make grants for school clothing and allowances to assist children of low-income families to remain at school after 16. Such provision varies greatly from place to place. The 1944 Act also required every education authority to provide a cooked midday meal for any child requesting it. Charges for these meals could be reduced or set aside for children from low-income families. The 1979 Education Act repealed the original requirement; local education authorities must now make such provisions as seem requisite (not necessarily including cooked meals). Children of families in receipt of supplementary benefit or Family Income Supplement are currently entitled to free school meals, although it is planned to replace this entitlement with a cash allowance under the social security scheme to be introduced in 1988.

4.65 The education system also provides for children with special educational needs. One example of this is the provision of special schools for children with disabilities. The 1944 Education Act gave local education authorities responsibility for the education of all handicapped children, with the exception of those regarded as ineducable who remained the responsibility of the Ministry of Health. Deaf, blind, epileptic, aphasic or physically handicapped children were to be educated in special schools, while other children with disabilities — the partially sighted or partially deaf, educationally subnormal and diabetic were to be educated in ordinary schools if adequate provision could be made. Subsequent legislation has placed on local education authorities the responsibility for the education of all children, and has encouraged the integration of children with special needs into ordinary schools. The 1981 Education Act proposed the creation of special units on the site of ordinary schools, or special classes within the schools. Depending on the degree of disability, children from the special units or classes might share lessons or activities with the other children in the school. Some children with special needs might be placed in ordinary classes full-time. Additionally, changes have been made in the way needs are assessed, with greater stress being laid on the involvement of the parents.

4.66 Another group of pupils who may have special educational needs are children from ethnic minority groups. During the 1960s, special programmes were set up to provide help with English for the children of immigrant parents. Although primary immigration has declined, children from homes where English is not spoken may need help. In recognition of the need for extra staff to carry out this teaching, grants have been made under the Urban Aid Programme towards the additional salaries for staff in schools with a large proportion of children from ethnic minority groups.

4.67 Achievement is strongly influenced by social circumstances. It is not easy for children from low-income families, who live in inadequate, overcrowded housing, whose parents may have had limited education, to do well. Their surroundings may limit their opportunities, even in small ways such as not having privacy to do homework. Resources have been made available for education in socially deprived areas to try to meet some of the needs of these children. During the early 1970s, Educational Priority Areas were established and money was set aside for extra expenditure on school buildings and more staff. Nevertheless, a child's home background is still the strongest determinant of achievement.

SHORTCOMINGS OF THE EDUCATION SYSTEM
4.68 One aim of the 1944 Education Act was that everyone should receive the education best fitted to his or her need. The needs of some children, however, are not met as well as they might be. There is particular concern, for example, about the lack of achievement among children of West Indian descent. Generally they are under-represented in selective schools and over-represented in units for educationally subnormal children.[25] The Swann Report, published in 1985, showed that, as a group, these children are less likely to do well than all other children, including other ethnic minority groups.[26] They achieve fewer examination passes and are less likely to obtain jobs on leaving school. It is not clear whether this under-achievement can be attributed to differences between the cultures and forms of language of home and school, or to the attitudes and expectations which teachers may have towards children of West Indian descent.

4.69 Second, the architects of the 1944 Act hoped that social disparities would be diminished and that social mobility would be improved. Education mirrors the inequalities in society at large. A study published in 1980 showed that while all have benefited from changes in the education system since 1944 in terms of achieving some qualifications, there are still serious disparities between the achievement of children from professional and managerial families compared with the rest.[27]

4.70   Finally, one key principle of the 1944 Education Act was that every child should receive the best possible education, irrespective of parental income. This is being seriously undermined by current trends. Recent public expenditure cuts in schools have, in some cases, been made good in part by parental contributions. In the 1985 Report from Her Majesty's Inspectorate of Schools, it was stated that 'While parental and other contributions have long been a feature of schools, the increased scale and range of these have served to widen the differences in the levels of individual resources available to individual schools.'[28] Children in schools in areas of high unemployment, high social deprivation, are likely to be denied adequate access to text books and equipment, while children in more favoured areas stand to gain. Thus the inequalities in achievement will be perpetuated, and maybe magnified.

The Private Sector of Welfare Provision

4.71   The comprehensive development of welfare services by the state since 1945 has not replaced private provision. Beveridge, in designing his system of social security, envisaged that private provision would always remain, and was concerned not to stifle individual initiative. Private health care, education and personal social services have always been available to those who chose, and could afford, to pay for them. Private house ownership has expanded dramatically since 1945. In recent years, increasing attention has been paid to the possibility of people providing for themselves, rather than relying on services provided by the state. Particular areas of growth in private provision in recent years have been in pension plans, health insurance and education. Some services traditionally run by the state have been taken over by the private sector. A good example of this relates to some catering, laundry and cleaning services in hospitals.

4.72   It is sometimes thought that there is a neat division between the public and private provision of services. While this is for the most part true, there are areas of overlap where public services depend on private contributions, and private services receive contributions and subsidies from the state. People have, for a long time, paid for certain services provided by the state, though often at a subsidised price. The home-help service, school meals, prescription charges provide examples. Second, the private sector does not operate independently of the state. The private health care sector depends on people trained within the public sector as does private education. Funds are also transferred from public funds to the private sector. For example, the Department of Health and Social Security makes allowances to residents of private nursing homes, and local authorities make extensive use of private bed and breakfast accommodation to house homeless families.

4.73   However separate the public and private sectors seem to be, the private sector cannot escape the regulatory function of the state, whereby standards are set for the services provided. Residential homes, for the elderly, handicapped or children, as well as schools, and hospitals, are regulated through qualification requirements and by inspections. Private pension schemes and sick pay arrangements must conform to standards laid down by the state, and so can be fundamentally affected by changes in legislation.

4.74   It is difficult to envisage that private provision could ever replace public provision in its entirety. There are some activities undertaken by the public sector which are not attractive financially, and thus will be avoided by the private sector. Private health insurance schemes may restrict the range, duration, or cost of care covered in order to avoid the unlimited expenditure required by long-term care. Nevertheless, it is likely that the private sector will continue to receive attention as a means of diminishing the cost of welfare provided by the state.

The Voluntary Sector of Welfare Provision

4.75   The provision of welfare is not limited to the public and private sectors. There is a long history of individuals and groups who have been moved to help people experiencing times of crisis. This section reviews different kinds of voluntary activity, together with its strengths and weaknesses. As might be expected within the context of this report, we have paid some attention to the part which Christians have played in the voluntary provision of services. This is not to diminish the importance of all contributions, whatever their motivation.

4.76 There is not one of the major areas of welfare provision from which Christian involvement has been absent. The foundation of schools and hospitals, the provision of low-rent housing, the care of orphans, elderly people, single mothers, prisoners and ex-prisoners, and handicapped people, are all areas in which Christians have been actively engaged, sometimes in a pioneering role. The burgeoning of such activity came in the latter half of the nineteenth century as people became better informed about the extent of poverty, and the magnitude of the inequality between the rich and the poor. There was an increasing recognition that distress was not, in most cases, the fault of individuals but was dependent on economic and social factors outside their control. The scale of the problems put their solution beyond the competence of the voluntary societies. Throughout the twentieth century increasing demands were made on the state to intervene. The introduction of old age pensions in 1908 and the unemployment insurance scheme of 1911 were in some measure a response to this pressure. Gradually a partnership between the state and the voluntary sector developed as the state began to employ social workers to work in parallel with existing provision. It was assumed by some in post-war Britain that the enhanced provision of social security, together with the establishment of the NHS and the implementation of the 1944 Education Act, would render the existence of the voluntary organisations superfluous. This withering of voluntary activity did not occur; some activities were maintained and different forms of action grew in response to changing social needs.

POST-WAR DEVELOPMENTS IN THE VOLUNTARY SECTOR

4.77 A new development in the voluntary sector since 1945 has been the growth of agencies giving advice to people, particularly on the complexities of state welfare provision and how to obtain the correct benefits, and on the procedures for contesting decisions relating to benefit entitlement. A good example of such activity is provided by the Citizens' Advice Bureaux.

4.78 Pressure groups have also developed to challenge government policies on behalf of particular groups of people. So, for example, the Child Poverty Action Group was set up in the mid–1960s to campaign on behalf of low-income families. Similarly Shelter was set up initially to draw attention to the plight of people who became homeless, and to the standards of accommodation offered to them by local authorities. Its campaigning role has extended to all aspects of housing policy, especially housing shortages and the problems of disrepair.

4.79 Mutual-help groups have been set up by people experiencing special difficulties, who have found support in sharing their experiences with people in similar situations. The Association of Carers, for example, was set up in the late 1970s to give support to people looking after severely disabled or elderly people. Such work cannot be necessarily divorced from a campaigning role. The Association of Carers has urged successive governments to recognise the importance of the role that carers play and give them more practical help. Groups for lone parents, people with specific handicaps or illnesses have also multiplied within the last 25 years or so.

4.80 With the growth in local groups, the need for co-ordinating bodies has grown. As early as 1919, the National Council for Social Services was set up to co-ordinate the work of local councils. This became the National Council for Voluntary Organisations in 1980 which plays a vital role in the dissemination of information to voluntary organisations, and in representing their interests to Government.

4.81 Finally, many kinds of voluntary activity have been encouraged by grants made available from both central and local government. Housing associations, many of which are church-based, are largely dependent on central funding from the Housing Corporation. Central government grants tend to be given to national bodies, though there are local exceptions, while local branches of voluntary organisations may be helped by local authorities and health authorities. Most local authorities, councillors and officials, welcome the voluntary sector and the service it provides for the community. A contrary view, not often expressed, is that local authorities should not support voluntary organisations in the belief that bodies which may be less publicly accountable should not have the power to give or withhold services or to dispense funds affecting people's lives.

STRENGTHS AND WEAKNESSES OF VOLUNTARY PROVISION

4.82   A major part of the work of voluntary organisations is still the provision of services. Voluntary activity to some extent complements statutory provision by providing services which might not otherwise exist. Pre-school play groups, some kinds of counselling services provide examples of this. The Samaritans, the Mothers' Union 'Message Home' scheme, the Terrence Higgins Trust for people with AIDS, all help to fill important gaps in statutory provision.

4.83   Another strength of the voluntary organisations is that they are more free than statutory services to deal with issues in new ways. So, for example, the Children's Society has established a series of Family Centres in disadvantaged areas which aim at giving support to the whole family, not just the children, and encouraging people to work together to deal with the problems of their local communities. Sometimes practices developed in the voluntary sector are taken up by statutory provision. The most striking example of this is provided by the growth of the hospice movement, where the patterns of care for people facing death have been adopted as a model for developments within the framework of the National Health Service.

4.84   Some voluntary agencies provide the same kinds of services as can be found in both the public and private sectors. People may be able to choose between alternatives. The Church Army and the Church Housing Association, for example, manage hostels for homeless people. Alternatives are available, provided by the DHSS and private concerns, but those do not, for the most part, offer the same standards of accommodation or care.

4.85   The term 'voluntary organisation' conjures up a picture of unpaid people joining together for particular purposes. Many organisations, however, employ professional workers such as housing managers and social workers, who work together with people who give their time and ideas on an informal basis. It is estimated that about 15 per cent of the population are engaged in some kind of voluntary work. Tensions may develop between professionals and volunteers, but such arrangements do make for a high degree of public participation in determining what kind of services should be provided and how they should be organised. Often volunteers support statutory services. Thus, the Meals on

Wheels service, often operated by the WRVS, is a vital component in the range of services which allow people to live in their own homes, rather than in residential care.

4.86 It was said earlier that voluntary organisations had the opportunity to operate flexibly and be innovative. They have, on occasions, been rigid in their styles of operation and slow to recognise that their particular service was no longer relevant to social needs. There is no guarantee that voluntary effort will match need since provision is often patchy. Neither is there necessarily any co-ordination between agencies, although this does exist in many places. In addition, the financial arrangements for voluntary societies mean that they nearly always live with insecurity about funding. Much time which might better be devoted to the main task has to be spent in fund-raising.

4.87 In summary, the voluntary organisations are able to develop new activities, experiment with different styles of care, provide alternatives and tap the resources of a large number of people. The weaknesses are that they may be resistant to change, may not work with other agencies and may meet some needs only partially. The voluntary sector does, however, provide an important alternative to both public and private sector provision and forms a major strand in the mixed economy that now provides welfare services.

Conclusion

4.88 The first part of this chapter looked at the achievements and shortcomings of the welfare services provided by the state. It was concluded that, in spite of serious deficiencies, there is much for which to be grateful. The biggest concerns range round the extent to which those in need experience multiple deprivation — in health, housing and education, as well as being dependent on low incomes.

4.89 State welfare provision does not exist in isolation and in the second part of the chapter, the contributions of the voluntary and private sectors were outlined. In spite of the importance of these, the part played by the state is still pre-eminent. Whether or not this balance should persist is a large part of the debate about the welfare state. The next chapter explores the arguments in some detail.

Chapter 5

THE BREAKDOWN OF AGREEMENT

5.1 The achievements of the welfare state are, we argue in Chapter 4, considerable. In the last ten years, however, criticisms and doubts have been expressed by most elements in the political spectrum, and from many other groups. The general agreement which existed in the post-war years, that the principles behind the welfare state were sound, and that it was on the whole 'a good thing', have given way to debate. This debate is both healthy and confusing. It is healthy because it is important to look critically at what is happening and to have a clearer sense of what we want. But it is confusing because of the many different philosophical positions that have emerged and because of the complexity of the political and economic choices that have to be confronted.

5.2 This chapter tries to make sense of where we have got to, 40 years on. It looks at why consensus is no longer as solid, first pointing out some general themes and then looking at four of the major critical perspectives. The accounts are necessarily only brief summaries, deliberately outlining with a broad brush rather than going into close detail. But they are important for understanding why there is a debate at present, and why in the mid-1980s the meaning and future of the welfare state are key political issues.

Some Reasons for the Debate

5.3 'Can we afford it?' and 'What effect does it have on the economy?' are probably the most serious and common questions asked about our welfare provision in the 1980s. High economic growth levels in much of the post-war period enabled a relatively painless growth in services, and a nearly universal acceptance of the major role of the state in welfare provision. But with the recession, the consequent rise in unemployment and decreasing proportion of wage earners in the population, the national expenditure on welfare provision has increased while the

79

country's traditional wealth-creating base has been eroded. It is not surprising, therefore, that some have blamed the welfare state for Britain's economic difficulties: it is alleged that higher taxes have reduced incentives and fuelled inflation. The relationship between economic and social policy has become strained, and the welfare state has become an easy target. As the Monmouth group which wrote to us put it, 'We are keenly aware of the gathering storm-clouds over the welfare state, with inadequate resources to meet ever-increasing demands'.[1] At the same time more questions have been asked about how we allocate resources, both within the social welfare budget, and within the national budget as a whole.

5.4   'Does it do what it set out to do?' is another question, and points to increasing debate about the effectiveness of the welfare state, and indeed about what it should be trying to achieve. We have already emphasised some of the achievements and real progress of the last 40 years. But it is increasingly clear that some objectives associated with the legislation of the 1940s remain unfulfilled and that some were perhaps too ambitious.

5.5   The basic issues here are to do with aims and objectives. What is the welfare state for? Is it about the relief of poverty? Is it about preventing poverty? Is it an expression of the reality of human interdependence? Or is it about the redistribution of wealth and the construction of a more equal society?

5.6   One view argues that the welfare state was always intended to offer a minimal subsistence level to all in need. In other words the aim was to provide a collectively woven safety net. In this case, the welfare state exists to relieve the most extreme forms of remediable hardship. It is to be judged by whether it does this effectively, preventing people's income falling beneath a certain point. Others argue that the aims of the welfare state always had more to do with the cohesion of the nation as a whole and should function as a well organised insurance scheme writ large. In this case the welfare state is rightly concerned with poverty but only as one of its aims. It should also be a mechanism for redistributing wealth and income, and reducing inequalities.

5.7   On either view the welfare state cannot be said to have achieved its aims. The safety net has holes in it and the distribution of wealth and income has not changed significantly. It is also argued that the rich have benefited as much or more from the provisions of the welfare state than have the poor. Even within the Health Service, where the most universalist principles have operated, the outcome is still unequal. The Black report showed, for example, that the risk of death before retirement is two and a half times as great for manual workers and their wives as it is for professional workers and their wives.[2] Similar comments could be made on housing and education programmes. As Lesslie Newbigin remarked in the 1984 Gore lecture: 'In spite of all the housing programmes of successive governments, a walk through any of our cities will quickly demonstrate the gulf that divides the housing of the affluent suburbs from that of the inner cities'.[3] So even for the supporters of the welfare state, it sometimes seems easier to find the shortcomings rather than celebrate the achievements.

5.8 The welfare state is also criticised for the way in which it works and the effect it has on those who use it most. As the administration has grown it has become very difficult for people to participate in decisions about resources which directly affect their lives. The most obvious example of this is the process of claiming social security — often one which leaves people feeling devalued and baffled. A debate has also arisen about dependence. Here the argument is that the state has taken over many of the functions and responsibilities which the individual should properly carry, and that the professionalisation of caring undermines a person's initiative, self-respect and independence as well as the need for neighbourliness. The debate is well illustrated by two of our responses. One diocese commented that 'a trend which has been observed, particularly in our residential work, is the emergence of a "welfare state generation". Young people show an increasing dependence on state services and have expectations of what they should receive by right. With these expectations comes a reluctance to make provision for the future, and to place a value in improvements achieved by their own efforts.'[4] On the other hand one response stated firmly, 'I don't believe... that the welfare state has undermined people's sense of moral obligation towards family or neighbour. I do believe the way our society has developed has made it more difficult for families and neighbours to assume responsibilities they once did, e.g. they are often far away from home; old people are living longer and the degree of constant care is often greater as a result; the design faults of the tower blocks built in the 1960s have led to isolated people with no neighbours.'[5]

5.9   Another criticism is that the welfare state has not changed in line with the changes in social trends. In the words of one diocesan response, 'The structures of the welfare state are not sufficiently flexible to provide for developments to meet the changing needs of society: e.g. unemployment benefit is not designed to cope with high levels of long-term unemployment; there is a growing need for conciliation services; the legal aid system could be related to welfare provision'.[6] We do, the argument runs, live in a very different world from that of the 1940s, and the challenges for public policy are immense. Roles and expectations of women have changed, patterns of employment and family life have altered. But, the argument continues, our systems are still fundamentally the same and increasingly inappropriate to the 1980s.

5.10   Alongside these criticisms must be placed the evidence of considerable public support for many aspects of the welfare state. A health authority initiative to close a local hospital, or an education committee decision that a school is too small to be viable, can provoke fierce opposition and an impressive level of community lobbying and organising. When a resource is threatened the public reaction is often to summon all possible time and energy to save it. The problem with such an approach is that it is essentially defensive; if the fight is successful the status quo quickly returns and the real changes which may be necessary are not tackled.

5.11   Recently too there have been more attempts to find out what the public thinks about health and welfare services. The results are interesting on two fronts. First, it seems that a large group of the population does understand the direct links between taxes and services, and would be willing to pay more in taxes in order to finance some of the public services more generously. Second, attitudes to poverty and those who live on benefit are becoming less punitive; we seem to be becoming less willing to blame people for their situation.[7]

5.12   Within these general themes, it is possible to identify several critiques adopted by particular groups. Here we select four for closer attention: the Feminist Critique, the New Right Critique, the Marxist Critique, and a critique which emphasises the local, participatory dimension. We conclude each section with a brief evaluation of the position.

The Feminist Critique

5.13   The feminist critique of the welfare state is nothing new. In 1943 a Women's Freedom League Pamphlet came out entitled *The Woman Citizen and Social Security: A Criticism of the Proposals in the Beveridge Report as they affect Women.* But it is only in the last fifteen years that feminists have turned their attention more vigorously to the mechanisms of the welfare state. They have focused on three connecting areas: the assumptions about the family and the role of women; the structures of the health, education and personal social services as employing bodies and agencies which offer services; and the way that services are organised.

5.14   The welfare state, feminists argue, is founded on values and assumptions which limit and control women's lives. It relies on a rigid and increasingly archaic model of the family. Women are seen by the state as simultaneously dependent, and themselves the major carers for dependants within the family. The man is assumed to be the breadwinner; he is expected to be in (or looking for) paid employment. The woman's primary role by contrast is to care for dependants — the disabled, the elderly, and children. The man's 'family wage' should support a wife and children too. The woman is assumed to receive financial support from the man she lives with if their relationship is (or is like) that of husband and wife.

5.15   Some of the most notorious examples of the welfare state giving different value to the contributions of men and of women have been in the organisation of social security. Until recently the Invalid Care Allowance, for example, was particularly discriminating. This was available to everyone caring for a disabled person for at least 35 hours a week with little or no income from earning, except married or cohabiting women. The effect was clear: a man giving up work to care for a disabled partner or relative would be 'compensated', a married or cohabiting woman would not. A second example concerns the

83

implementation of 'Care in the Community' policies. There is growing evidence that an enlighted policy of enabling a greater number of mentally ill and mentally handicapped people to live outside institutions depends in practice on the willingness of women to be the unpaid supporters and carers, and to live with great tensions and responsibilities. Fran Bennett of the Child Poverty Action Group comments that 'When the welfare state mentions "the family", women are never far from its mind.'[8] The same could be said of 'community care'. As has also been pointed out, community care usually in practice means care by the family; care by the family usually in practice means care given by women.[9]

5.16 The second area of concern for feminists is the disappointment that in so many respects the welfare state merely reflects and reinforces structures of patriarchy, that is, a social system which accords status, leadership and decision-making to men. For example, inequalities remain in occupational patterns. The statistics available on staffing in the personal social services show clearly that women dominate the front line of welfare and that men are far more likely to find themselves in decision-making management positions. So in 1976 83 per cent of social work assistants (the lowest social work grade in social services departments) were women; 9 per cent were directors of departments.[10] Even in a profession like social work which expanded very rapidly in the 1970s, employment patterns have tended to follow the same trends as in the health and education sector, with the same hierarchy of pay and status. Fewer tasks in residential care can be harder than caring for severely mentally frail and physically dependent elderly people but it is noticeable that this task is nearly always carried out by women (often black women) and is very poorly paid.

5.17 The other strand of the feminist discussion about structure is that of participation. Women are far more likely than men to experience poverty and to find themselves using the services of the welfare state. Single parent households, which despite additional child benefit are often in real hardship, are usually headed by women. There are more elderly women than men living in poverty because women live longer, but also because they are less likely to have occupational pensions and other forms of financial security.[11] As *Better Services for the Mentally Ill* points out, women have an estimated one in six chance of entering a psychiatric hospital during their lives.[12] The corresponding figure for men is one in nine. At any one time almost 60 per cent of the population of British psychiatric hospitals are women and 44 per cent of them have been in hospital for over five years.[13] Yet despite their greater use of many of the welfare state services, women have had little chance to shape them in accordance with their needs. Some feminists would put this even more strongly. Elizabeth Wilson argues that 'One way of looking at social policy would be to describe it as a set of structures created by men to shape the lives of women'.[14]

5.18   The third area concerns the process by which the welfare state gives help, and reflects the growing realisation in all branches of welfare services that how you give help is as important as what you give. The women's movement has used the well-worn but nonetheless crucial slogan 'the personal is political' to look inwards without shame and make connections between the facts and figures about resources and the experience of being a patient, client or claimant. Questions have been asked about stigma, labelling and about the power vested in the hands of the 'caring professionals'; be they doctors, social workers, even social security officers. Other styles of work have been explored in Women's Aid Refuges and Rape Crisis Centres. Gradually the feminist debate has become more reflective. With the rise of mass male unemployment, fewer simple assertions are made now that economic independence will achieve all. More thought is given to the subtle and complex connections between consciousness, gender and self-confidence. As Fran Bennett suggests 'After twenty years in which the proportion of women with dependent children who are in paid employment has doubled, we must also be more conscious of new areas of vulnerability for women — such as the increasing impact of the "double shift" (the job and the home) with all its accompanying stress.'[15]

5.19   What value is there in the feminist critique? How can it be of importance to Christians in thinking out their response to welfare? The argument that sexist assumptions permeate welfare state policies and impinge significantly on the lives of many women seems undeniable. The feminist voice has made a difference by drawing attention to basic injustices and by giving women users a greater confidence to express their needs. Women have led the consumerist revolt in the NHS, particularly in the field of ante-natal care, and in the struggle to increase the choices open to women about how they wish to deliver their babies. One book after another has encouraged women and men to tell their stories.[16] Some important steps have been taken. The welfare state has attempted — though without great enthusiasm or success — to outlaw sex discrimination and unequal pay for equal work. A number of social security regulations have been changed following pressure from the European Economic Community, and though the actual gains of such changes are sometimes questioned by women, the principle is important. For example, since 1983/84, if the woman has been the 'main breadwinner' for the previous six months, she can claim supplementary benefit for herself and the man she lives with too. And, in a similar vein, if she is the full-time worker in a couple and the man is not, they can claim Family Income Supplement as an addition to her low earnings should they have a child or children.

5.20   The feminist critique is not of course, and would not claim to be, the whole story. Some of its greatest successes — in pointing out discrimination against women, and in giving status to personal experience — have been shared by other groups. In some respects it rests uneasily on a community of interests defined by gender; equally powerful alliances have been formed along the lines of race, sexual orientation and class, and those alliances have voiced their criticisms of the welfare state. It is now for example very well documented that ethnic minority groups are less likely than others to receive certain services (such as home help, good housing) and conversely are over-represented in some areas where the state has a more controlling function (for example a disproportionate number of black people enter psychiatric hospital compulsorily and a disproportionate number of black children are received into local authority care).

5.21   Uncomfortable though it may be, the feminist critique of the welfare state is important for the Church. First, it forces us to look honestly at some of the words which slip easily and unobtrusively into many Church conversations — words like 'caring' 'service to others' and 'family'. We find ourselves challenged to examine our assumptions, and be clear about the costs as well as the joys of day to day commitment. This may encourage a more realistic attitude to what caring involves: much could be done in our own communities to offer practical and emotional support to the many men and women who look after dependent relatives and 'put a brave face on it' rather than ask for help.

5.22   Second, the feminist critique can help us to see the sheer variety of ways in which people now live. It often appears that the Church goes hand in hand with the welfare state in assuming family patterns which are not now the experience of the majority. Further that the Church gives a kind of moral backing to this mythical norm, so that those who do not fit (for example single parents) experience not only material hardship and social stigma but also moral disapproval. We may need to learn to use the word 'family' much more carefully, and perhaps sometimes not at all.

5.23   Third, the feminist critique of the welfare state as an institution challenges us to give some of the same rigorous attention to roles within Church structures and to take action on the basic injustices which prevent the full contributions of women being welcomed. Lynne Segal looks forward to the day when 'those same family values of love, care and commitment which, if seen as the individual responsibility of women, are oppressive, could extend beyond the confines of gender and home to become an essential part of a society which would liberate us all'.[17]

5.24   Fourth, it alerts us to the truth that the ultimate test of the welfare state is what it means to people, not how it seems to professional staff, academics and politicians.

The New Right Critique

5.25   One of the most important sets of criticisms of the welfare state is made today by those who have come to be known as 'the New Right'. Drawing on the work of people such as Milton Friedman,[18] F.A. Hayek,[19] and Robert Nozick,[20] New Right critics have become influential in political and academic fields, and have struck chords with the public. The literature is large, and it is important to recognise the diversity of views covered by the term 'New Right', but the general themes are familiar. Indeed one of the most interesting features of the debate is the frequency with which some of the people on the left wing of the political spectrum, using a different philosophical approach, arrive at some of the same conclusions.

5.26   The New Right lays great stress on individual liberty as the basis for a healthy society. People should be free to pursue their own good in their own way. They must have responsibility for their own achievements and rewards and can decide whether or not to make the grade. Fate, accidents of birth can be surmounted. Individuals are in charge of their own destinies and can achieve economic and social success by effort, determination and initiative.

5.27   The state should do as little as possible in order not to infringe the liberty of the individual. What it must do is the minimum necessary to ensure that people and their property are not violated by others. It should limit itself, therefore, to providing those circumstances in which people are as free as possible to set their own targets and determine their futures. The welfare state has been severely criticized by the New Right precisely because it conflicts at several points with the principles of maximum individual liberty and minimum state involvement.

5.28   First, welfare states involve the compulsory redistribution of property rights usually through the tax system. Giving a right to welfare gives a person in need rights to the property of the better-off. It may be that people will help others in need, but there should be free choice about such altruism or charity. People in need do not have a *moral* claim on the better-off, which they might have if their plight resulted from injustice. They are in need, however, as the result of bad luck and those who have had better luck are not responsible for providing for them.

5.29   Second, advocates of the New Right position argue that a welfare state with its system of benefits removes from people the incentive to achieve, to take responsibility for their own destinies. It is not the responsibility of the state to assist those who have been unwilling to help themselves.

5.30   The New Right argues that individual liberty is infringed by the welfare state in yet another way. In respect of their own personal needs, individuals may well be obliged by the existence of a state system to make regular payments for protection or social insurance which they might choose to obtain elsewhere, or perhaps relinquish at certain stages of their life-cycles. A good example is provided by the national insurance scheme. Individuals might prefer to buy insurance cover in the private market, or even to take the risk of being uninsured, using their contributions for other expenditures.

5.31 The New Right wishes individuals to be able to spend their income as they themselves choose. A centralised scheme of welfare provision deprives tax-payers of their own resources and channels them in bureaucratically determined ways. Services provided by local and central government and by large voluntary organisations tend to give people little or no choice about the type of service which is provided. They contribute through taxation to public services but then, in practice, have little control over how the money is spent. What is provided may not be what consumers want but what professionals and bureaucrats think they want. Public provision is therefore inevitably unresponsive to human needs and wishes. The New Right contrasts this situation with a market system where consumers choose what they want from a range of goods and services provided by producers who will stand or fall by their ability to offer the products which consumers want.

5.32 The New Right also believes that the state should not determine what is good for people, since this is to deny the equality of all citizens. Again the welfare state violates this principle. Officers of local and central government often do not perceive their role as particularly powerful and may be only too aware of the frustration of their position, the delays and internal arguments. But they nevertheless make crucial judgements about need. In Friedman's words, public services 'put some people in a position to decide what is good for other people. The effect is to instil in the one group a feeling of almost god-like power; in the other a feeling of childlike dependence.' Individuals also come to believe that the state is the main source and provider of welfare services. Other systems of welfare — the family, the community, the voluntary sector — are neglected.

5.33 The New Right also argues that there are disturbing implications for the economy and for government in having a strong welfare state. Financing the welfare state involves such high rates of taxation that incentives are often destroyed, inflation fuelled and investment damaged. Furthermore, once a government takes on more than a minimum role in welfare it is laying itself open to pressure from many different groups. Since it depends on support for remaining in power it cannot deny concessions and is weakened by its subservience to vested interests. True political democracy is weakened.

5.34   It is believed that the large-scale state provision of welfare is inefficient. The absence of competition can lead to inefficiencies, the waste of national resources, a lack of innovation and experimentation. The welfare state is not subject to the two basic disciplines of the market — close concern with costs and sensitivity to consumer preference. Most people are unable to purchase alternative services since the income they might have used has been taken in taxes and used for state provision. Those who work within the welfare state tend to be those most in favour of it, because they benefit from it.

5.35   The New Right belief that private provision is more effective economically, creates fewer threats to political stability and has less damaging consequences to individuals and families has undoubtedly made a contribution to the debate about the welfare state. What is the value of the New Right's critique? The commitment to individual freedom, to personal responsibility and to enabling people to gain control over their own lives so that they may make their own choices is important. If welfare policies undermine the capacity of people to be responsible for their lives and circumstances and if such policies create too much dependence on the state and its bureaucracies, those policies are not achieving the best for people. The concerns about the uniformity and remoteness of state provision must be taken seriously; it is significant that such concerns are shared by many groups who would place themselves at very different points on the political spectrum.

5.36   The New Right, similarly, is not alone in worrying about the frequent discrepancy in status between those who are paid to administer public services and those at the receiving end. Finally, the emphasis on the centrality of the family, the community and the voluntary sector is an important reminder of the huge amount of daily caring that does go on quite outside statutory provision.

5.37   Many New Right thinkers acknowledge that there must be provision for those whose income falls below an absolute minimum. They should be assisted without undermining the incentives to achieve. The criticism is made, however, that the New Right is over-optimistic about its reliance on market forces to produce a healthy society. A principle of respect for people cannot imply an indifference to whether their basic needs are met. In order to pursue their own good lives, people must, first of all, be given the means to survive. The New Right has been questioned about whether its policies are likely to prevent increasing poverty, and growing inequalities in such areas as income, education and health. Doubts are also expressed about the validity of relying on market forces to provide care: can market forces operate compassionately in situations where human beings are at their most vulnerable, for example, adults with long-term mental illness, children with multiple disabilities? It is also pointed out that many of the New Right's proposals appear to be based on an idealised view of the extent of the altruistic forces in society.

The Marxist Critique

5.38   Marxists are a very varied group. As the aim here is simply to convey the central thrust of the Marxist critique of the welfare state some generalisation is appropriate. Marxists do, inevitably, vary in the emphasis they place on some elements of the critique rather than others.

5.39   It is important to point out immediately that Marxists are ambivalent about the welfare state. Marxism is essentially about revolution, not reform. Those who are in the business of revolution must beware of reformism — change which seeks simply to ameliorate particular ills and is not part of an overall strategy for changing the nature of society. Marxists stress the importance of understanding how and why the welfare state has developed. It should not, they argue, be seen as a simple humanitarian response to manifest social need. Rather, its development must be seen as a response to the needs of the economic system — capitalism — and to working class pressure because class conflict is a central fact in such societies. Capitalism needs healthy and educated workers if it is to be efficient and productive. It needs contented workers, efficiently socialised to capitalist norms and values — hence social policies to support the family and the school. Above all, the state needs to appear as a concerned, caring, even-handed body, not as the capitalist state which Marxists argue is what it is. It needs legitimation, and the provision of welfare can give the state the image it wants and needs. They argue that welfare provision is to be seen in part as a ransom offered by capital to labour to buy acquiescence to an inequitable economic and social system.

5.40   What Marxists seek to do is to make sense of the welfare state within capitalist society from their particular ideological perspective. The constraints which Marxists see surrounding a welfare state in a capitalist society lead them to stress that social services cannot change society. They may represent genuine gains for the working class but they are gains within a particular pattern of economic and social relations which by its nature is, and remains, exploitative. This is because the social services essentially deal with symptoms not causes. The National Health Service, for example, is intended to provide care for the sick but it does nothing about the system which creates sickness through poverty, unemployment, bad housing, pollution, stress and so on.

5.41   Marxists see the social problems with which the welfare state seeks to deal — poverty, unemployment, ill health, homelessness, bad housing and so on — as the product of the very nature of capitalism, not of some remediable malfunctioning. Social services are seeking, therefore, to resolve problems which are insoluble without broader and much more radical economic and social change.

5.42   Another important emphasis in the Marxist critique of the welfare state is to stress the conflicts about values which afflict welfare states in capitalist societies. To survive, our economic system requires certain values — individualism, competition, self-help, independence. A welfare state, on the other hand, requires a concern for meeting need, altruism, co-operation, and sharing. The contrast and possible conflict between these two sets of values is obvious. They are likely to be sharply at odds with the values required to initiate and sustain an adequate welfare system.

5.43   Marxists welcome the welfare state as offering the working class political movement tangible, immediate collective goals to fight for. But they are anxious that the achievement of some modest gains and the papering over of the more obvious cracks of capitalism may take the drive out of the political movement for broader and deeper change. History shows — not only to Marxists — that reformist parties tend to slide from commitment to socialism towards the less arduous pursuit of social reforms.

5.44   What is the value of this critique of the welfare state? First, it locates analysis of the welfare state firmly in the context of a broader economic, social and political analysis of society. It emphasises that the welfare state can only be understood as part of the particular society in which it is set.

5.45   Second, the Marxist critique alerts us to the limitations of the welfare state. It is constrained by what are judged to be the needs of a healthy economy — punishment for failure, benefits sufficiently below normal earnings to preserve incentives, benefits available on conditions which maintain work discipline, overall levels of expenditure and methods of financing which keep redistribution from rich to poor at an acceptably low level.

5.46   Third, this critique helps us to understand better some of the reasons why the achievements of the welfare state have been less than its creators had hoped. Inequalities of health, of access to health services, of educational achievement and so on survive because economic and social constraints are more powerful than the supposed equality of services offered by the welfare state.

5.47   In sum the Marxist critique provides little in the way of prescriptions for curing the ills of the welfare state or improving it but it does help us to understand more clearly some of the constraints within which it operates and the reasons for some of its shortcomings. It is challenging in its refusal to be content with piecemeal social reform and its insistence on the wider historical framework. But this challenge leads to limitations: the reluctance to examine social policies in detail or to attend to particular trends, or emerging needs. The argument that welfare services merely 'paper over the cracks' of a doomed system ignores the crucial assistance which many welfare services bring to people's everyday lives, and can actually reduce the incentive to improve them.

The Local, Participatory Approach

5.48   Since the 1960s a critique of the welfare state has evolved for which it is almost impossible to find a satisfactory title. The approach emphasises the value of the local, participatory dimension in welfare. The most famous exponent of this approach is probably Ivan Illich, author of bestselling books such as *Deschooling Society*,[21] and *Limits to Medicine*.[22] But the approach has a more pragmatic and mainstream line in, for example, Roger Hadley and Stephen Hatch's book *Social Welfare and the Failure of the State*.[23]

5.49   Let us look first at Illich's critique. One of his central criticisms of schools and medical treatment is that they lead people to confuse process and substance. People come to think that schooling is education; they mistake medical treatment for health. What develops is dependence on professional intervention. People's own ability to teach themselves to take care of their health wastes away. They look to bureaucracies and professionals to deliver education and health.

5.50   Not only, Illich argues, is this damaging to people because they lose their capacity for independent, self-reliant action. It is also a recipe for failure. Schools are not the most important educational institutions. Most of the important things we learn, and need to learn, are learned outside school. The health service cannot make us healthy. What makes us healthy or unhealthy is how we live, the nature of our work, our social relationships. Heavy demand for specialised, professional health care is, in Illich's view, an indication of a society pursuing unhealthy goals. Indeed traditional health care can actually create sickness — in Illich's term, iatrogenic illness.

5.51   What Illich says about health and education illustrates a general anxiety among this group about whether state social services actually deliver what they promise — education, health or personal social services, satisfactory housing. That anxiety is based on three things: the nature of the services, the way in which they are customarily organised, that is bureaucratically, and the key people staffing them, professionals.

5.52   Followers of this school of thought are concerned about increasing professionalisation in social welfare for various reasons.

They see it as creating or exacerbating problems of social distance between the clients and those providing the service. They see it as leading to, and encouraging, professional definitions of problems rather than allowing clients to define their own problems. They see it as contributing to a neglect of people's capacity for self-help. Illich has gone so far as to talk about 'disabling professions'.

5.53   These critics worry about the bureaucratic organisation of welfare services because they see it as leading to remoteness and impersonality and an inability to respond flexibly to individual needs. Bureaucracy they see as a result of the increasing size of local government units or organisation. They argue that large institutions begin to pay a great deal of attention to the welfare of those who work within them, rather than those for whom the service was established. They see small as beautiful because it avoids these inevitable disadvantages.

5.54   Underlying these critiques of professionals and organisations is the view that the goods which the welfare state seeks to deliver are just not amenable to delivery in this way. A typical example is the kind of regular assistance which many people require to live independently. Social services departments simply cannot deliver the kind of service which families, friends and neighbours can supply, because of the nature of the care that is needed and because of the nature of public organisations. Instead the approach stresses the potential and importance of the educational, health-supplying, care-delivering mechanisms of everyday life. They are seen as more effective, more efficient and more acceptable than publicly provided services.

5.55   These critics see the welfare state as the expression of what they term 'top-down welfare' — some people, professionals and bureaucrats, deciding what other people need and delivering it to them as, when and where they think best. They call for the involvement of clients and consumers in decisions about the nature and pattern of provision, both as a democratic right and as a way of ensuring that services are actually directed to needs as defined by users. They see hazards in large-scale, professional, public welfare. This leads them to argue for a decentralised, local, system where the number of professionals is kept to a minimum. This does not lead them necessarily to reject state funding, but rather to emphasise the importance of as much local control as possible.

5.56　This perspective contains serious challenges to many of our present organisations. It offers a warning about current and future trends in organisation and delivery and the dangers of those who offer help becoming remote from those who receive it. It asks important questions about power and decision-making and emphasises that users of services should have a far greater say in what they are offered. It gives great value to the informal networks of care, self-help groups, and local organisations, and asks how public provision could relate to these more creatively. In doing this it questions how the apparatus of the welfare state relates to the welfare of society as a whole, and how professionals and statutory services can play a creative role without 'deskilling' or 'disabling' ordinary people and local communities.

5.57　But it can be argued that the critique does not take into account the fact that organisations and bureaucracies are crucial for welfare in the twentieth century. They may not work perfectly, but they are vital. Furthermore, the analysis can, as it is suggested, become a new dogma: small is not necessarily beautiful; small can be experienced as oppressive and limiting.

Summary

5.58　This chapter has examined a number of criticisms of the welfare state, made predominantly from different ideological perspectives. While in many respects the evaluations are very different, there are two important points about which there is a great deal of agreement. First, several critics argue that people come to depend on services provided by the state, rather than looking at what they could do to help themselves. People, argue these critics, lose their capacity for independent action.

5.59　Second, there is concern about how services are made available to people who need them. There are criticisms of the scale of administration of the services, the apparent inability to respond easily to local or individual requirements. Professional people may assume that they know what people need in the way of services, without involving those very recipients in the making of such decisions.

5.60   It is these very important dimensions that need to be taken into account when alternative schemes of welfare provision are discussed.

Chapter 6

PAYING FOR WELFARE

6.1   At the centre of the debate about the future of the welfare state is the cost of supporting it. It does, as we shall see, cost a great deal of money. Our discussion takes place against the background of a serious debate about matters of philosophy and basic principles conducted by economists. The introduction which we have offered to the thinking of the 'New Right' and of 'Marxists' is part of the background to this debate. It is an argument about whether large-scale expenditure on welfare helps or hinders the long-term growth of the economy and the production of wealth.

6.2   There are some who argue that we must be prepared to afford a state system of welfare provision and, indeed, that by expanding social expenditure (especially in terms of investment expenditure on education and health) we can stimulate the economy. Some argue the opposite: that to revive the economy, to create growth and wealth, we must reduce the size of the welfare state because the level of taxation it requires debilitates the economy, and because if large-scale public expenditure is met by taxation and heavy borrowing it is inflationary and cannot be sustained. They argue that the reduction in government expenditure, coupled with the reduced taxes which will be made possible and the increased incentives this will provide, will help to rejuvenate the economy without at the same time allowing inflation to undermine the benefits thus gained. While the first school sees the expansion of social expenditure as being the means of stimulating the economy, the second school argues that the economy can and should be stimulated through reduction in government expenditure.

6.3   It is important to be aware of this basic discussion as a background to this chapter. We now set out, as simply as possible, how welfare services are paid for, where the money goes, and draw some conclusions. Three questions emerge:

1. What does social welfare cost the nation?
2. How is social expenditure paid for?
3. What are the wider economic issues raised by expenditure on social welfare?

Expenditure on Welfare

TOTAL SOCIAL EXPENDITURE

6.4   Figure 5 shows the pattern of social welfare spending since 1959. The data are in £ thousand million at 1984 prices. Expenditure in 1984 on social welfare was just over £80 thousand million, which was almost 25 per cent of the Gross Domestic Product (GDP).

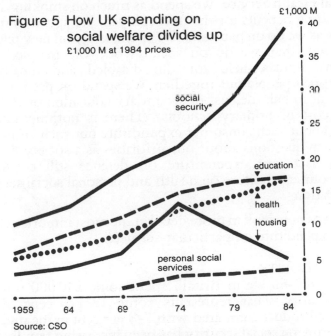

Figure 5 How UK spending on social welfare divides up
£1,000 M at 1984 prices

Source: CSO

*including contributory benefits (such as unemployment benefit and retirement pensions) and non-contributory benefits (such as child benefit).

6.5   At just under £40,000 million in 1984 social security was by far the most expensive social service. It absorbs nearly 50 per cent of the total social welfare budget and 30 per cent of all public spending. Spending on education and health is roughly equal at £15,800 million and £16,600 million respectively in 1984. Both have doubled from 1959 to 1984 but education spending has now levelled off. In contrast direct public expenditure on housing has shown a dramatic reduction since the mid-1970s, the only service to show a significant fall. Personal social services absorb relatively small amounts of money and, after a rise in the early 1970s, expenditure is virtually on a plateau.[1]

6.6   The sums involved in supporting the welfare state are clearly very large. However, comparing expenditure on welfare with other kinds of expenditure may help to put it into perspective. As a nation we spend only slightly less on alcohol than we do on the National Health Service. We spend as much on smoking as we do in providing benefits for the unemployed. We spend as much on our cars as we do on pensions. We spend more on new televisions and stereos than we do on social work, old peoples' homes, children's homes, help for the disabled and the mentally handicapped people put together. We spend on pet food a sum equivalent to half the cost of secondary education or two-thirds of the cost of primary schools.[2] There is nothing inherently wicked about such consumer expenditure but such comparisons raise sharp questions about our priorities as a society. One final salutory fact: our expenditure on defence still considerably exceeds our expenditure on health and personal social services or on education.

6.7   Let us now look in more detail at the most important features of our expenditure on particular services.

SOCIAL SECURITY
6.8   In 1985-86 we in Britain spent some £40,000 million on social security. That represents some 12 per cent of Gross Domestic Product compared with 7-8 per cent in the mid-1970s. Expenditure on social security has been increasing rapidly both in cash terms and as a percentage of GDP. Figure 5 shows that social security costs more than twice as much as health or education, which is very different from what the picture was ten years ago.

Table 1

MAJOR ITEMS OF SOCIAL SECURITY EXPENDITURE 1985–86 (estimated) (GB)		
Contributory Benefits	£million	
Retirement Pensions	16,782	
Widows Benefit	812	
Unemployment Benefit	1,597	
Invalidity Benefit	2,373	
Sickness Benefit	296	
Industrial Disablement	396	
Maternity Allowance	173	
Total Contributory		22,510
Non-Contributory Benefits		
War Pensions	560	
Attendance Allowance	668	
Disablement Allowance	228	
Mobility Allowance	430	
Supplementary Pensions	1,008	
Supplementary Allowance	6,200	
Child Benefit	4,531	
Family Income Supplement	136	
Housing Benefit — Rent Rebate	2,292	
Rent Allowance	776	
Total Non-contributory		16,904
Total Benefit Expenditure	39,414	
Admin. & Miscellaneous Services	1,807	
Total	41,221	

Source: Cmnd 9702.-II, Table 3.15
N.B. Major items only are included here, and therefore totals do not add up exactly.

The biggest single item in the social security budget as Table 1 clearly shows is, quite properly and fairly, retirement pensions — nearly £17,000 million in 1985-86 — something over 40 per cent of the total social security budget. Fifteen years ago pensions absorbed about 47 per cent of social security spending, but the percentage has dropped as other benefits have increased in importance. Personal and corporate expenditure on occupational pensions, of course, has also increased.

6.9   The next largest item is supplementary allowances — that is supplementary benefit to non-pensioners — costing over £6,000 million. This has increased sharply in recent years with the rise in unemployment. In the three years between May 1979 and May 1982 the number of unemployed people getting supplementary benefit trebled and the number has gone on rising. Ten years ago supplementary benefits to the unemployed accounted for 3 per cent of social security spending. Now it is well over 10 per cent.

6.10   Child benefit is the third biggest element in the social security budget costing over £4,500 million in 1985-86. It is expensive because all children receive it — some 12 million currently — but the number has fallen by over a million since 1979-80 as the child population has dropped.

6.11   Other important elements in the social security budget are housing benefit costing around £3,000 million, invalidity benefit for the long-term sick and disabled at over £2,000 million, unemployment benefit costing £1,500 million (less now in real terms than in 1981-82 as fewer of the unemployed meet the contribution conditions) and supplementary pensions at just over £1,000 million.

6.12   Another way of analysing social security expenditure is to look at it in terms of the groups benefiting from it. Fifty per cent of all social security expenditure goes on the elderly. About 20 per cent goes on support for families with children. Some 17 per cent goes to the unemployed. The remaining 13 per cent goes to help the sick and disabled. The dominance of the elderly is striking but not surprising given the large numbers of elderly people in the population. Again, lest elderly people should be wrongly accused of being a burden on the welfare state, it should be remembered that the majority of them have made substantial cash contributions towards their pensions in advance.

HEALTH
6.13   In the early 1950s the National Health Service absorbed between 3 per cent and 4 per cent of GDP. It now takes just 6 per cent of a vastly greater national product. Expenditure has to grow simply to maintain standards primarily because of increased numbers of elderly and very elderly people but also to meet the increased cost of new treatments. It is roughly eight times as expensive to provide health care for people over the age of 75 as it is for people aged 16-64. And the over 75s are about two and a half times as expensive as people aged 65-74.[3] It should be noted that this heavy expenditure on elderly people is in large measure due to the number of beds which they occupy in geriatric, mental and other hospitals which are not necessarily appropriate to their needs.

6.14   Where does the money go? About 70 per cent of all NHS expenditure goes on hospitals. General Practice, excluding the cost of drugs — costs only 10 per cent of the cost of hospitals. Drugs are a major element in the cost of Family Practitioner Services — amounting to nearly half the total cost of General Practitioner, Dental and Opthalmic Services. Charges for prescriptions are paid by only 30 per cent of patients and cover well under 10 per cent of the total bill for pharmaceutical services. On the other hand in 1984-85 some 30 per cent of the cost of dental services was covered by charges. But together Family Practitioner Services take only about a quarter of total NHS spending.

6.15   There are powerful pressures operating to increase spending on health care. Developments in medicine make possible new treatments. New drugs are discovered. The survival of many who would have died in the past increases demand and need; so do higher expectations of medicine and a reluctance simply to endure discomfort or disability. These pressures are apparent in all industrial countries. What the NHS seems to have done more effectively than most other health care systems is to control the potential cost explosion produced by these trends and developments.

6.16   It is staff who constitute the expensive element in the NHS. About three-quarters of the average health authority's current expenditure goes on staff salaries. The largest single element in that budget — nearly 50 per cent — is nursing salaries. Doctors only absorb about 10 per cent of the staffing bill.

6.17 The NHS does not guarantee equality of access to care. Studies undertaken in the early 1970s showed that the older industrial areas of the north and west, less prosperous rural areas and parts of Greater London were at a disadvantage in terms of health provision when compared to the rest of the country, particularly the south-east. In 1977 'target' allocations were worked out for all Regional Health Authorities — what the DHSS thought regions *ought* to receive on the basis of various assumptions. Some regions were found to be 10 per cent below their spending target, others as much above it. Matters had improved by the mid-1980s, with more regions clustering near the target but there were still regions almost 10 per cent above their targets and others seriously below.

6.18 Efforts have been made, too, to increase expenditure on 'Cinderella' groups like the elderly, the mentally ill and mentally and physically handicapped people. There has been some success, but it is still better to be an acute rather than a chronic patient.

HOUSING

6.19 Housing finance is immensely complicated. Housing has borne the brunt of cuts in public expenditure since 1974 but public expenditure remains considerable. Though the present pattern of expenditure is widely criticised, proposals that changes should be considered arouse fierce protests from those who see their political or financial interests as threatened.

6.20 There are four main types of public expenditure on housing.

(1) There are general subsidies from the Exchequer to local authorities, new town corporations and housing associations to help to meet the costs of servicing loans and maintaining property. The aim and effect is to reduce rent levels below what they would otherwise be. Between 1980 and 1985 general subsidies to the public sector in England fell from £2,000 million to under £1,000 million. Government policy has been to reduce the subsidy given to local authorities, to end any subsidy from the rates and to increase council house rents to bridge the gap.

(2) For individuals there are means tested cash benefits in the shape — mainly — of housing benefit. Housing benefit has replaced rent rebates, rent allowances and rate rebates and is available primarily to local authority tenants and the tenants of private landlords. In 1985-86 it cost £3,000 million.

(3) There are various types of capital expenditure by central government and by local authorities for new house building by local authorities, new towns and the Housing Corporation and for home improvements in the public and private sectors. These amounted to rather less than £2,500 million in 1985-86. Over the period from 1974 the volume of expenditure has fallen by about 50 per cent.

(4) Finally there is tax relief on mortgage interest which cost the Exchequer some £4,750 million in 1985-86 — an increase of 35 per cent over 1984-85. We shall discuss the tax allowance welfare state later on in the chapter but tax relief on mortgage interest is such a central element in public support for housing that it must be mentioned here if the reality of the unco-ordinated nature of public expenditure on housing is to be grasped fully.

PERSONAL SOCIAL SERVICES
6.21   Personal social services are small scale in expenditure terms, costing rather less than £3,000 million per year by the mid-1980s. Since social services departments were set up in 1971, expenditure has, however, increased relatively rapidly — but from a very low base. Real spending doubled between 1970 and 1975; it increased by rather more then 10 per cent between 1975 and 1980 but by only some 3 per cent between 1980 and 1985. As with the NHS, expenditure needs to increase simply to maintain current standards of service. Predictably there is disagreement about the annual increment required. The DHSS thinks that 2 per cent is adequate. The Association of Directors of Social Services argue that 4-6 per cent is a more realistic figure. Academic experts judiciously reckon that 3-4 per cent is what is needed. The need for more resources simply to maintain standards underlies the argument as to whether or not there have been cuts in services. The government talks of increased expenditure. Local authorities talk about cuts in services. Both can happen at the same time when needs are increasing.

6.22   The most expensive activity for social services departments is the provision of residential care. That absorbs nearly half the typical department's spending. Day care absorbs about 15 per cent. Community Services such as home helps, meals on wheels, aids and adaptations, telephones take about the same. Social workers account for only around 12 per cent of spending. Administration, research and miscellaneous services absorb the remainder of the budget.

6.23   An analysis of expenditure on the personal social services by client groups indicates that here too the elderly take the largest proportion, absorbing over a third of social service department expenditure. Children and families come next with about a quarter. Identifiable expenditure on other groups is relatively tiny. The mentally handicapped do best but because of their long-term needs rather than because the level of provision is high.

EDUCATION

6.24   Expenditure increased from just over 3 per cent of the Gross Domestic Product (GDP) in the early 1950s to a peak of 6.3 per cent in the mid-1970s. Since then the trend has been downwards, partly because of the fall in pupil numbers, partly because of government policies to reduce public expenditure; and so in 1985 expenditure was rather less than 6 per cent of GDP. Even so, expenditure per pupil has increased in real terms in recent years.

6.25   Around 60 per cent of educational expenditure goes on schools. Some 30 per cent goes on further and adult education and universities. Further, adult and higher education cost more than primary education. Universities alone cost about half the total bill for primary schools — even excluding the cost of student grants. Elderly people make few claims on the formal education services.

6.26   Roughly half education expenditure goes on teachers' salaries. Less than 1 per cent goes on books and only about 2 per cent on equipment. Schools are administered by local education authorities with varying degrees of enthusiasm and commitment. In 1981–82 the highest spending London boroughs spent a third more per secondary pupil than the lowest spenders. In Metropolitan Districts the gap between high and low spenders was even greater. On the specific item of books and equipment, where education authorities might be judged more able to influence current spending, and less bound by existing premises or particular patterns of staffing, the discrepancies between high and low spenders were of the order of 70-80 per cent in all types of local education authority.[4]

How Do We Pay for the Welfare State?

6.27   At one level the answer is obvious: through taxation of various kinds and through charges for services received. If we are looking at who actually pays and what they pay, then the answer is much more elusive. Table 2 shows the relative importance of the main sources of government tax revenue in 1984-85.

Table 2

SOME MAJOR SOURCES OF REVENUE AS A PERCENTAGE OF TOTAL TAXES 1948-1985 (UK)			
	1948	1972	1984-85
Income Tax & Surtax	32	31	27
National Insurance Contributions	8	15	19
Tobacco, Beer, Wines & Spirits	25	10	6
Local Authority Rates	8	11	10
Value Added Tax	–	–	14

Source: *The Economist* 17 September 1983. Financial Statement in Budget Report 1984-85. HM Treasury, 1984.
Figures do not add up to 100 per cent as these are the main sources only.

6.28   Most people would, if asked, probably have guessed at income tax as the most important source of tax revenue but they would probably have guessed a larger percentage than the 26.5 per cent which it actually yields. Over the years, in fact, income tax has produced a declining percentage of total tax revenue.

6.29   The burden of income tax has also shifted significantly. Put simply: a two child family started paying income tax twenty years ago when its income reached average earnings; the same family today starts paying income tax at about half the average earnings. Most families on Family Income Supplement, a means-tested benefit for poor working families, now pay income tax. This is an administrative absurdity, irrespective of any concern for equity and fairness in taxation.

6.30   Since 1979 a central aim of government has been to ease the tax burden of the better off. There has been a decline in the numbers of taxpayers paying income tax at rates above standard rate. There have been adjustments to rates of tax, to thresholds and to allowances which mean that the total yield of income tax in 1985-86 is £6,000 million lower than it would have been if the 1978-79 rates still applied and only the required statutory changes had been made. The top 2 per cent of earners received 30 per cent of that £6,000 million. The bottom 20 per cent of tax payers received a mere 4 per cent.

6.31   Income tax began life as a tax on those on middle incomes and above. As late as 1939 only one in five of the workforce paid it. Now it is four in five. Income tax has become virtually a universal tax which bears heavily on incomes scarcely above supplementary benefit levels. The unemployed, for example, now contribute some £600 million to income tax through the taxation of the unemployment benefit.

6.32   National Insurance contributions have more than doubled as a percentage of tax revenue since 1948. Successive Chancellors have grasped that increases in national insurance contributions are less unpopular than increases in income tax because they are connected in people's minds with the establishment of a right to benefits and because the burden is shared by employer and employee. In fact, because of the ceiling on the income on which contributions are levied (£265 per week from October 1985) they take a larger percentage of the income of many of those on lower incomes than of those on higher incomes.

6.33   Local authority rates now contribute a slightly smaller proportion of tax revenue than they did twenty years ago. There have been no dramatic changes. Current government concern cannot be understood in terms of changes in the contribution of rates to general tax revenue. The central problems with rates are clear and obvious. As a tax on property values rather than income, rates take no direct account of ability to pay. They are likely to be regressive, that is to say they take a smaller proportion of the income of the richest one-fifth of households than of the poorest fifth. This is modified to some extent by rent rebates, and the degree to which they are taken up. But the plan in the new Social Security legislation requiring everyone to pay at least 20 per cent of their rates will mean that the beneficial effects of rate rebates are reduced. Rates also have to be increased to generate increased income whereas, in a situation of rising incomes, whether real or the product of inflation, income tax yields a fiscal dividend without any actual increase in tax rates by the Chancellor of the Exchequer.

6.34 Value Added Tax now produces 14 per cent of tax revenue. Purchase Tax, which it replaced, never produced more than half that proportion so VAT has meant a major increase in the contribution of indirect taxation to total taxation. The classic argument against such taxes is that they hit the poorer hardest because they take no account of ability to pay. Thus at first sight it might be thought that such a tax would be regressive.

6.35 However, a study by E. Davis and J. Kay[5] finds that, because basic items such as food and fuel, which consume a larger proportion of lower income budgets, are zero-rated (as are housing and children's clothing), VAT turns out to be a slightly progressive tax, though not everyone would agree with this conclusion. Since 1979, there has been a clear Government policy to raise more money from indirect taxation.

6.36 In 1984–85, Corporation Tax, a tax on company profits, contributed only 8 per cent of total tax revenue. This was because, prior to its reform in 1984, companies received large investment allowances and grants (to encourage investment and job creation) which they could set against their tax liability. Since the reform, the average effective rate of Corporation Tax is higher, and marginal effective rates are more uniform across different types of investment. Consequently, revenue can be expected to rise.[6]

6.37 What is strikingly absent from Table 2 is any significant contribution from taxes on wealth and capital. Capital gains tax and capital transfer tax have, in fact, declined in importance over the years. In the early 1970s they produced over 7 per cent of Inland Revenue taxes. Ten years later they generated only 2½ per cent. Furthermore the 1986 Budget has effectively removed wealth taxation, since the new inheritance tax looks weaker.

6.38   It is generally accepted as a principle of taxation that the broadest backs should bear the heaviest burden; that those with higher incomes should not only pay a larger *amount* of their income in taxation but should also expect to pay a larger *proportion* of their income in taxes.

6.39   What proportion of income do different groups pay in direct and indirect taxation in Britain? The poorest 10 per cent pay little in the way of direct taxes but pay nearly 30 per cent of their income in indirect taxes. The richest 10 per cent pay only some 16 per cent of their income in direct taxes and something between 20 per cent and 25 per cent in indirect taxes.

6.40   The question of whether the British tax system is truly progressive is a subject on which economists disagree but the contrast between the richest and the poorest is stark and inevitable and the recent changes in taxation have served to increase rather than reduce it.

6.41   Income tax in Britain starts at low levels of income and begins at a rate, now 29 per cent, which is higher than in most comparable countries. And national insurance contributions have to be added to that 29 per cent. Since October 1985, contributions are 5 per cent on incomes between £35.50 and £55 per week, 7 per cent on incomes between £55 and £90 per week and then 9 per cent on incomes up to £265 per week.

6.42   In recent years tax rates on the highest incomes have been reduced to 60p in the pound. The better off tax payers also benefit more than the less well off from a wide range of tax reliefs and allowances which enable them very significantly to reduce their tax liability so that a mere 3.5 per cent of tax payers in Britain pay tax at rates above standard rate. The idea that the better off are heavily taxed in Britain is one of those myths which serve to obscure a reality which is very different.

Winners and Losers from Welfare State Spending

6.43   The general conclusion about winners and losers is plain. 'Most public expenditure on the social services in Britain', (and elsewhere) Julian Le Grand concludes at the end of his major work *The Strategy of Equality*, 'is thus distributed in a manner that broadly favours the higher social groups, whether "higher " is defined in terms of income or occupation.'[7]

Professionals, employers and managers receive up to 40 per cent more NHS expenditure per patient than semi-skilled and unskilled manual workers.

The top fifth of earners receives nearly three times as much public expenditure on education per household as the poorest fifth.

In housing, direct expenditure on council housing and benefit scheme favours the poorer. Mortgage tax relief is clearly, however, of greater benefit to the better off. Le Grand's conclusion is that, at the end of the day, public expenditure on housing favours the better off with the richest 20 per cent of households receiving nearly twice as much as the poorest 20 per cent.

Social security spending is clearly and predictably most redistributive to the poorer. In 1981 40 per cent of social security expenditure went to the poorest 20 per cent and a further 30 per cent went to the next 20 per cent. The shares of the two top groups were both less than 10 per cent of total expenditure.

6.44   This distribution of expenditure on social services is not difficult to understand. For a range of reasons — poorer services in poorer areas, greater problems of access to services, loss of earnings involved in visiting the doctor, difficulties of communication — the poorer make less, and less effective, use of health services relative to need.

6.45   In education, expenditure is roughly equal between social groups up until the age of 16. Then, as education becomes more expensive, it becomes more socially selective as working class children leave the system. The most expensive parts of education, namely higher education, remain a predominantly middle class preserve.

6.46   It is mortgage tax relief which is decisive in the inequitable distribution of public expenditure on housing. Tax relief is not granted on loans over £30,000. (This figure has not kept pace with inflation. The previous limit of £25,000 was set in 1974.) The larger the mortgage up to the limit of £30,000, the greater the value of the tax relief received. For anyone paying income tax at higher rates tax relief is, of course, worth more.

The Tax Allowance Welfare State

6.47   For 30 years academics have talked about the tax allowance welfare state. They mean by this the direct benefits which accrue to individuals from a range of tax reliefs and allowances. In those 30 years tax reliefs and allowances have become ever more costly to the Exchequer and an ever more significant element in the provision of welfare. Detailed costings now appear in the annual public expenditure White Papers — a clear recognition that tax allowance should be seen as part of the total cost of the welfare state.

WHAT DOES IT COST?
6.48   Table 3 shows some of the major reliefs and allowances and their costs in 1985-86. The sums involved are large and they have been increasing. The Exchequer is clearly forgoing very large amounts of tax revenue.

Tax relief on mortgage interest — £3,500 million in 1984-85, £4,750 million in 1985-86 — vastly exceeds expenditure on housing benefit, which now stands at £300 million. This increase reflects high interest rates, rising house prices and an expansion of owner occupation.

The exemption of most owner occupied housing from capital gains tax probably costs the Exchequer about 80 per cent of the cost of the housing benefit scheme.

Tax relief on pensions is difficult to calculate but probably costs the Exchequer a sum equivalent to the total cost of the supplementary benefit scheme.

Such reliefs may be an appropriate way of pursuing particular social objectives. What is crucial to a balanced appraisal of social expenditure is that such forms of 'expenditure' are considered and evaluated alongside other more obvious elements of welfare spending.

6.49   All those liable to income tax may benefit from tax allowances because of the way they reduce or eliminate an individual's liability to tax. But the benefits are worth much more to some than to others. For example, those with larger mortgages will obviously benefit more from mortgage tax relief. So will those with higher incomes who might be liable to income tax at rates above standard rate save for the ability to reduce their taxable income through reliefs and allowances.

Table 3

COSTS OF SOME INLAND REVENUE TAX RELIEFS AND ALLOWANCES 1985-86

	£million
Married man's allowance (includes £440 million cost of the difference between the married man's and single person's allowance)	12,900
Relief for	
employees' contributions to occupational pension schemes	1,400
investment income of occupational pension schemes	3,500
lump sum payments to pensioners	1,000
retirement annuity premiums	325
Life assurance premiums (where contract made before 14 March 1984)	640
Mortgage interest	4,750
Exemption from capital gains tax on sales of main residences	2,500

Source: *The Government's Expenditure Plans 1986-87 — 1988-89*, Cmnd. 9702-II, Table 2.24.

6.50 Only 3.5 per cent of the 24 million tax payers pay income tax above standard rate, thanks to the reduction in taxable income made possible by the tax allowance welfare state. In 1979-80, the latest year for which full figures are available, nearly a third of all reliefs against income tax went to people with incomes above £10,000 a year even though they formed under 8 per cent of all taxpayers. As regards mortgage interest relief, in 1983-84 70 per cent of the total relief went to tax payers with income over £10,000 p.a. Those with incomes over £20,000 received almost 20 per cent.

6.51   The tax allowance welfare state is a vastly expensive benefit system. It assists a great many people with low as well as high incomes but it is of most benefit to the better off. What is striking, too, is the lack of government willingness or ability to control such expenditure. Public expenditure on housing has been cut drastically since 1979, by over 50 per cent in real terms. The cost of tax relief on mortgage interest, however, has roughly doubled in real terms in the same period.

6.52   The tax allowance welfare state can also be challenged on the grounds that it does not reflect contemporary needs. When most wives were not gainfully employed a special tax allowance for married men made sense. In a world in which a majority of married women work outside the house it does not, and it costs the Chancellor of the Exchequer (i.e. the taxpayer) £4,400 million per year. Such a sum could finance an increase of £8 per week in child benefit, though any such redistribution would need to be done over time. If the aim of the Married Man's Tax Allowance is to help families with the cost of rearing the next generation, then resources should be directed to where they are most needed — families with children. If the aim of the Married Man's Tax Allowance is different — for example, to encourage people to marry rather than cohabit, then different considerations would apply. The moral and practical issues which have to be faced here are complex, but it is hard to argue that the present position is satisfactory.

6.53   Another result of the proliferation of tax reliefs and allowances is that less than half of all recorded income in the UK is now subject to tax. Because so much income escapes taxation, the income which is taxed has to be taxed more heavily. Given the greater ability of those with higher incomes to benefit from tax allowances, the result is a greater tax burden on those with lower incomes.

6.54   Certain important conclusions emerge from this review of what is spent on the welfare state and how such spending is financed.

Welfare spending is not simply, or in many services primarily, of benefit to the poor. The better off get a more than proportional share of a number of expensive services.

To talk about public expenditure on welfare without including the tax allowance welfare state is to ignore a major cost to the Exchequer and an important source of welfare.

A more logical distribution of benefits and taxation is desirable. For example, the present pattern of tax relief on mortgage interest needs to be reviewed.

Change is possible. The tax changes since 1979 have returned annually to the pockets of the better off sums which could make an important difference to the quality of our social services and the quality of life of the poor. As noted above, a redistribution of the £4,400 million cost of the Married Man's Tax Allowance could enable a massive assault on family poverty. A simple redistribution according to need of the monies government currently spends on assisting individuals with the cost of their housing via tax relief and housing benefit could be a major step forward in social justice.

As a society we need not be trapped forever in the anomalies of a system which has grown over many years and has not changed as society has changed. Change will need to be gradual, but it is both possible and desirable.

There is a substantial body of opinion in Britain in favour of spending more on welfare, and only a tiny minority who wish to spend less. Recent survey evidence suggests that only 5 per cent of the population want lower taxes and reduced social spending whereas over 40 per cent are prepared to pay higher taxes for better services.[8]

Conclusion

6.55   At the beginning of the chapter we mentioned briefly the fundamental disagreement about the impact of welfare expenditure on the economy at large. It is beyond the scope of this report to resolve such a broad and complex question, but it is important to be aware of it. It is obviously relevant to consider how the welfare state is paid for. This chapter has given a simple outline of how this is done at the moment, and made some suggestions about aspects of the present system that need to change. However, while economic policies cannot be ignored, that does not mean that economic theory must dictate the form and spirit of our welfare provision. The major decisions about the welfare state in this country were made immediately after a war which had left it drained materially. This was not, however, allowed to divert the nation from embarking on major social reforms.

6.56   The very confusion that exists about the impact of welfare expenditure on the rest of the economy shows that if the country is waiting for a united message from economists, it will have to wait for a long time. Decisions have to be made about the kind of society we want. Economic policies need to inform policy development, rather than determine it.

6.57   Of course the creation of wealth is important; of course means of reviving industrial and economic life must be sought; of course jobs need to be created in huge numbers. But the question remains: for what is that wealth to be used? The working party would argue that welfare, the well-being of all members of that society, cannot just be an incidental consequence of an economic policy but must be an integral part of the overall policy which decides in which direction our society should be heading. Only in this way can a proper relationship be reached between economic and social policy.

6.58   The welfare debate needs to be an integral part of the economic debate, not dependent on its outcome.

Chapter 7
FACING THE FUTURE

Introduction: Change and Continuity

It seems, just now
To be happening so very fast;

7.1   So writes Philip Larkin, in a poem called 'Going, Going', commissioned by the Department of the Environment in the early 1970s.[1] Here he is writing particularly of threats to the natural environment and of his fear that enormous damage will be done unwittingly. But he is also expressing a more generalised feeling of powerlessness, a bewildered uncertainty in the face of the many changes taking place around him and a longing for things to stay the same.

7.2   There is a sense in which much of this report so far has been about this tension between continuity and change. An earlier chapter summarised the major social trends. It looked at some of the important changes in the structure of the population, the reduction in the birth rate, and the rise in the number of very old people. Marriage and family patterns are also changing, with more marriages ending in divorce, and more one-parent families. But it was also pointed out that in many respects there is considerable continuity: marriage remains very popular and most children live with their natural parents. Other trends are the dramatic and serious rise in unemployment, particularly long-term unemployment, and the changing patterns of work. The current economic recession, the increased number of unemployed people, and growing numbers of one-parent families have meant that more people are living on or near the supplementary benefit level, and therefore in conditions of relative poverty. Many elderly people also live on low incomes. Underlying these trends are growing inequalities; between the high earner whose disposable income continues to rise and those living on benefit; between

117

different parts of the country; and between different areas of towns and cities.

7.3   Shifts in social patterns and the way we live now are not however the only changes this report has highlighted. Chapter 5 looked at changes in thinking and ideology over the last decade. It is easy to overestimate the degree of agreement there was in the 1940s about aims, objectives and means. But there was at that time enough shared commitment to provide the driving force for legislation which built a strong national base of collective responsibility in the shape of a wide range of welfare provision. Chapter 5 showed how that common mind has been weakened, and summarised the fundamental questions about the philosophy of the welfare state which have been asked recently in many quarters. For simplicity's sake four viewpoints were chosen — the feminist, 'New Right', and Marxist approaches, and a group of critics who cannot be easily defined but who stress the local 'community' dimension. It was noticeable that the four views refused to stay neatly separate. Often the boundaries between these seemingly very different philosophies were blurred. Among all the various perspectives some common criticisms emerged, especially the concern about bureaucracy, the desire for participation and the emphasis on giving more support to families and neighbours carrying out caring tasks.

7.4   A third area of change, closely connected to the above, is that of economic policy. Chapter 6 showed how the costs of the welfare state have risen considerably in recent years. Much of this is due to rising unemployment. The lack of dynamism in the manufacturing base has led to new pressures in the economy. All this has led to a much greater concern with the way welfare provision is to be financed.

7.5   One conclusion from these changes could be that the United Kingdom now looks so different from the 1940s that the only option is to start from scratch and construct a completely new system of welfare. That is not our view. From the evidence of Chapter 4 we believe that this country has a rich inheritance in traditions of welfare, and has achieved much over the years. There have been steady rises in minimum standards of social security, health, housing, social services and education. There have been gradual but encouraging changes in attitudes to some of the most vulnerable members of our community, such as people with mental and physical disabilities. Despite the shortcomings, each strand of the welfare state has contributed to achievements which cannot be disregarded. A good foundation has been laid and remains. The challenge for the rest of this century and beyond is therefore to build on the combined vision and pragmatism of earlier generations, paying attention to the particular needs, demands and constraints of present-day society, and listening to the comments which have been made by the welfare state's supporters and critics alike.

Facing the Future: Six Areas of Choice

7.6   The responses received to the Board's consultative document suggested that much of the present confusion about the welfare state comes from a failure to recognise both these changes and these achievements. Certainly great energy and determination, and a refusal to be complacent, are going to be needed to overcome the serious problems confronting the welfare services at the present time. For example, in the housing field, the sheer size of the bill for repairs to council housing alone is daunting. It has been estimated at £19 thousand million currently. For the housing stock as a whole the Audit Commission has noted that the repair bill could be as much as £30-£40 thousand million. In social security the number of people living near the poverty line seems to rise inexorably. In education, class inequalities remain unchanged and the under-achievement of young people of Afro-Caribbean origin in schools is all too well documented. In health the Black Report has shown how, despite some improvements in the general level of health, those at the bottom end of the social scale still die earlier and suffer from worse health. In the personal social services we are far more knowledgeable about the range of social services needed to support confused elderly people living at home and those caring for them, but the resources available to provide this support are under threat in many parts of the country. There are also dangers that the personal social services may simply be overwhelmed by coping with the casualties, unable to meet their responsibilities in matters of child abuse, acute mental illness and people with mental handicap returning to the community.

7.7   In the background of examples like these are major questions which are not going to go away. Here we select six of them, all large and complex, where choices have to be made.

THE RELATIONSHIP BETWEEN THE INDIVIDUAL, FAMILIES, NEIGHBOURS AND THE STATE

7.8   The question of the proper relationship between the individual, families, neighbours and the state is at the heart of nearly every choice made about welfare provision. In Chapter 5 we saw how the New Right, the feminists, and those stressing the local, participatory dimension, addressed the matter head on. From their different perspectives they all asked 'How much can families be expected to do? How can outside agencies help most effectively?'

7.9   This report has emphasised that most people's basic needs for physical care, support, and intimacy are met by themselves, their families and by informal carers. The evidence shows overwhelmingly that families do continue to care for their members whenever they can. Nevertheless, Chapter 3 made it clear that changes are occurring in the ways we live which must affect what families can be expected to do. The stereotypical 'cornflakes packet' family, with father in paid employment, mother in the home and two dependent children, represents only 1 in 20 of all householders at any point in time, but a substantial proportion of families will pass through this stage at some point in their lives. To say that families are somehow failing in their duty to elderly and handicapped people is to ignore the enormous increase in the size of these groups, the trends which make it immensely difficult for close contact to be maintained in many families, and, indeed, the numbers who have no close family. Any expectation that the individual will look to his or her own resources within the family and should only in exceptional circumstances need to turn to others flies in the face of the realities of the 1980s and 1990s.

7.10   Abstract discussion like this is quickly earthed by considering the choices involved in policies such as 'Care in the Community'. A large number of people with mental disorder and disabilities are currently being discharged from long-stay hospitals into independent, sheltered or hostel accommodation.

Most would agree that this in principle is a sound and enlightened policy, while adding serious warnings about the levels of funding and changes of attitude needed to implement it effectively. But the shifting of responsibility to families and neighbourhoods has wide implications. Properly managed and supported, an adult with mental handicap can discover a whole new life opening up. But inadequate support can lead to intense isolation and intolerable burdens on already stretched households, a deterioration in the quality of life, as well as pressures for which neighbourhoods are quite unprepared and to which they are unable to respond.

7.11 A further set of choices involves the role of women. Most policy decisions have assumed that women should, willingly or unwillingly, take the role of unpaid carers in the home, supporting the male breadwinner, caring for children and elderly relatives, and maintaining the home. Society has not chosen to value this work particularly highly, or to find ways of allowing men to play more of a part as fathers, sons, grandfathers and brothers.

7.12 At present the financial position of women is often jeopardised by the contribution they offer in bringing up children. Decisions have to be made about whether and how the central services of the welfare state should be developed to affirm the basic equality of women and men.

THE RELATIONSHIP BETWEEN PUBLIC AND PRIVATE PROVISION
7.13 Another crucial area concerns how services are offered and the proper balance between private and public services. As Chapter 4 pointed out, private provision is developing in all sectors. Although important principles are at stake here concerning the overall balance of provision, in practice the arguments are different in different policy areas. For example at one end of the continuum, more and more people see no contradiction between private home ownership (now at 61 per cent), and general support of the welfare state, while acknowledging the need for a strong public housing sector. At the other end of the continuum is health, where the issue is fiercely controversial. At the end of 1984 nearly 4.4 million people were covered by private medical insurance — nearly 8 per cent of the population. This compares with 1.6 million in 1966.[2] There are those who applaud the development of the private sector on the

grounds of choice and innovation. Others are concerned about its impact on the NHS and argue that a strong private sector in medicine is likely to be socially divisive and is parasitic for trained staff and for much of the more difficult treatment on the NHS.

7.14 One of the most striking growth areas is the establishment of independently run homes for elderly people. The number of residents in private homes has risen sharply since 1975 and doubled between 1980 and 1985. Reliable estimates show that there are about 70,000 places in private residential establishments in 1986, and that by the end of the decade this provision will outstrip that which is available from local authorities. Some of the growth over the past three years has been made possible through supplementary benefit board and lodging payments, but the main factor is the increase in capital reserves of many elderly people through home ownership, and the changing demographic structure.

7.15 There are therefore choices to be made about the mixed economy of welfare which we have inherited. Should we continue to have the bulk of services financed by taxation and administered through local government or should we encourage the growth of private provision?

7.16 In reaching decisions about an appropriate balance it is worth noting that the business failure rate of private care establishments and the high rate of turnover introduces a hazardous element for people when they are at their most vulnerable. Despite examples of excellent practice, the presence of untrained and unskilled staff is even greater than in the public sector, and in the least good homes the competition between profit and care can lead to lower standards which give cause for grave concern. In the period of expansion the long-established voluntary sector has suffered and the competition to fill new beds has driven up the proportion of the elderly population in residential care at a time when there is general agreement about the wisdom of policies aimed at keeping more elderly people at home. Similar concerns can be expressed about the public sector, but the controls and accountability are generally greater.

THE RELATIONSHIP BETWEEN PUBLIC AND VOLUNTARY BODIES
7.17 Chapter 4 described the important role of voluntary bodies

in the early years of this century, and the large contribution that Churches of many denominations made. It distinguished between volunteering (generally understood as giving time without payment) and those voluntary bodies which have paid staff, administration and often an extensive network of branches and local groups throughout the country. Amongst these are Church-based organisations, such as the Church of England Children's Society, Dr Barnardo's and the National Children's Home, which have developed exciting new roles. In general voluntary bodies have had an important role in pioneering services where the public is unaware of a need, such as the development of the hospices, or where the task is demanding and unattractive, such as hostels for homeless people.

7.18   Over recent years many voluntary bodies have developed a stronger political voice, though their financial position is often precarious. What is lacking is a coherent policy for the relationship between statutory and voluntary bodies. Some local authorities have devolved a great deal of responsibility to voluntary bodies; others have tried to develop a partnership with them through secure funding and support, and some degree of monitoring of the voluntary bodies in their boroughs. Others are suspicious of voluntary bodies and are reluctant to give them any place in the overall pattern of services. As one response to the Board's consultative document put it, 'Partnership between voluntary, private and statutory provision can produce creative tension or founder in misunderstanding'.[3] It has to be considered whether the voluntary agencies make a vital contribution to the overall network of welfare services, giving them a degree of flexibility and responsiveness which they would not have otherwise, or whether they introduce an element of divisiveness that makes the delivery of a fair and consistent service more difficult.

HOW MUCH PARTICIPATION?
7.19   We have moved away decisively from being a society which will accept paternalistic services. Users, carers, hospital patients, self-help groups, neighbourhood groups, pressure groups, have all made it abundantly clear that today's citizens expect to be able to participate in decisions which affect them. This is becoming well established in the housing field, but is much less developed in the health services and the personal social services. There is a

particular need to find ways of enabling those who are most powerless and vulnerable to have their say. But there is a tension between participation and rapid decision-making and action. We have to consider how far participation is practical and how far it would make the whole service more cumbersome.

7.20 The structure and scale of the services also needs reviewing to establish what form enables local people to participate most effectively. Of special relevance is the move to decentralise some services, especially housing and social services and to establish smaller offices.

UNIVERSAL OR SELECTIVE BENEFITS?
7.21 One of the most difficult questions is what the basic strategy in the face of poverty and need should be. In particular, should benefits be universal or should they be selective (that is 'targetted' to specific groups)? The best example of a universal benefit is child benefit. It is payable for all children. Its great strength is that the take-up is virtually 100 per cent and it reaches all families including those most in need. Because it is payable for all children there is no stigma attached to receiving it. But it is very expensive and it can be argued that many of the families who receive it do not 'need' it. Some argue that it is better to concentrate the money available on those most in need. One such benefit is Family Income Supplement, to be replaced by Family Credit. This is much cheaper, but those who wish to receive it must undergo a means-test. Take-up is only 50 per cent; many families who need this help are therefore not receiving it.[4] There is also a danger that this type of benefit may separate off those who are receiving it and make them feel like second-class citizens. The same is not true of selective benefits for those with particular needs, such as those receiving the attendance allowance, as these are assessed according to the person's disability rather than his or her income.

THE RELATIONSHIP BETWEEN TAX AND WELFARE BENEFITS
7.22 The introduction to this report explained our decision to choose a restricted definition of the welfare state, and to look at the five core services — social security, health, housing, personal social services and education. It has been hard to keep strictly to this definition, and this indicates just how intimately all these areas

124

are linked to other aspects of the nation's life. Nowhere is this more obvious than in the field of fiscal policy. There are some glaring anomalies. In 1981 four-fifths of families on Family Income Supplement (that is families who are among the poorest in the community) were also being taxed at the standard rate. In a more subtle way the tax and benefit systems are distorted by being considered separately. It is striking that if Government assistance is labelled 'a tax allowance' it is perfectly acceptable, indeed may not even be perceived as Government assistance; if assistance is labelled 'a benefit' it is likely to be perceived as a hand-out. So long as the two systems are kept apart it will be impossible to address effectively the fundamental question of the distribution of income and wealth in our society. This is too broad a question for us to consider in any depth in this report, but at the very least, searching questions will have to be asked about the justice of keeping the taxation system and the benefit system separate.

The Kingdom of God: Choosing Priorities

7.23   We face major choices about our priorities for welfare. The resources available inevitably affect those choices. Nevertheless it must be recognised that the proportion of the nation's budget that is allocated to welfare is a political decision about what matters most. Political decisions determine the relative budgets for defence and health spending. There is nothing fixed or magical about the choice of priorities which determine the present levels of expenditure on welfare.

7.24   How then are we to determine these priorities? We were given some clues to this in Chapter 2. Let us return to the central theological themes addressed in that chapter.

INTERDEPENDENCE IN HUMAN LIFE
7.25   God made us for one another. The fact that we need other people is not accidental but is essential to the human experience as God intended it. The interplay of giving and receiving is an integral part of a fully human life. We all depend upon one another. This experience of interdependence is, we believe, fundamental to understanding our social responsibilities. It is the context in which we can understand both our independence and our dependence.

125

It is easy to forget that those who have considerable independence still depend on others for their life and well-being. Likewise we can forget, in a divided society, that those who are highly dependent also have their own contribution to make to the welfare of the whole. They need to be supported so that they can do so. A real acceptance of what interdependence means leads into a proper understanding of community and so to an appreciation of the form society needs to take if we are to remove the barriers and divisions that tear us apart.

THE KINGDOM OF GOD: PRESENT AND TO COME

7.26 Christians live with a constant tension. On the one hand we believe that Christ by his death and resurrection has conquered sin and death; on the other hand, much sin, wickedness and suffering remain in the world. The reality of the kingdom of God, which is central to the teaching and ministry of Jesus, gives meaning to this tension. Christ has indeed lived and died and risen and has thus made the vital difference to women and men and communities who have accepted him. In Christ there is 'a new creation'. In this sense the kingdom of God has come. But the process is far from being complete. Christians live between the ages, impelled to look at their own lives, to be concerned with those who are the losers and to challenge the present order. In this sense the kingdom of God is still to come. The call of God's kingdom is not just addressed to individuals but to nations. Here and now in our common search for policies for welfare which offer hope, the kingdom reminds us of the need to take risks, of the need to recognise that our own work is never complete, and of the inevitable costs, especially to the more fortunate, of achieving new and better things.

JUSTICE AND OUR DUTY TO THE POOR

7.27 The biblical story constantly emphasises the responsibility carried by all for the ways society works. The righteousness of God has been revealed in the saving events recorded in scripture. In these acts we see the meaning of God's justice for the poor, the marginalised and the vulnerable. In human affairs we are called to show solidarity with the poor and to demonstrate God's righteousness and justice in the practical provision, both personal and corporate, which we make to restore the poor and disadvantaged to full participation in the life of the whole community.

7.28   These theological themes provide us with insights into the nature of community; into our responsibility to take practical action in the present in a way which offers hope for the future; and into the nature of our duty to the poor in the light of God's justice as witnessed to by the Christian tradition.

Towards Policy

7.29   We must now tackle the most difficult area of all. How should these insights be put into practice in Britain in the late 1980s? It is perfectly possible for people to agree about what they should be trying to achieve, but to disagree profoundly about how to do it. There is always a danger that means will be treated as ends. Thus the apparatus of the welfare state may be treated as sacred by some and any questioning of it viewed as betrayal of a commitment to justice for the poor; or the free market may be treated with equal reverence and any failure to maintain it in its purest form may be seen as a betrayal of respect for the individual. Such confusion is not surprising, for principles are no use without there being some means of putting them into practice. When people have committed time and energy over the years into finding a way of translating a vision into reality the form it has taken is invested with particular significance.

7.30   But the argument is not only about means. There is real disagreement about what the aims should be. For example there are different views on how far equality, or at least greater equality, should be an end. For those on the left greater equality is an end to strive for, whilst those on the right view egalitarianism with suspicion and think more in terms of setting a level below which no individual should be allowed to fall.

7.31   In order to present the multitude of choices in a manageable way five theoretical models are outlined below. They are necessarily simplified models. We describe these models to illustrate the possible approaches to providing welfare services. In reality the choices are not as tidy as this and in the policies that any particular political party offers there will generally be elements of more than one model. But they may help to clarify the directions in which we believe policy should go.

MODEL 1: PRIVATE ENTERPRISE AND CHARITY

7.32   The broad aim of such an option is to remove the state from areas of life beyond law and order, defence and the maintenance of contracts, and to restore responsibility for caring to the family and the individual. Social services, schools, and health care would be provided by private and voluntary agencies. Individuals and families would buy what they chose and doubtless would make provision by insurance schemes.

7.33   In a society divided between extremes of wealth, poverty, power and weakness, this model does not offer any hope for the restoration of justice. It is difficult to see how the poor and the powerless would achieve an acceptable quality of life. Moreover, the approach appears to work on the assumption that individuals and families possess all the basic resources needed for their lives. In reality we all depend on one another. None of us is self-sufficient. This suggests that there are responsibilities which must properly be assumed by society as a whole.

MODEL 2: THE STATE AS 'SAFETY NET'

7.34   This model aims to restrict the role of the state to that of providing a 'safety net', to prevent those unable to fend for themselves from falling into serious deprivation and poverty. Thus the state would offer a basic minimal back-up service for those who could not afford any other kind of health care, education, and social services. For the rest, provision would be by private and voluntary means through insurance schemes and specialist private agencies. Citizens would therefore be largely responsible for their own provision and the state would see that those on the margins were rescued from total exclusion. The state could have a further role of setting and enforcing minimum standards of practice and ensuring that people received a fair deal in any contract they made for a service. This model recognises that society has a limited duty to the poor. It restricts public action and provision to services directed towards members who have fallen below the minimum standard considered necessary for survival. It seeks to direct resources to specified needs.

7.35   In evaluating this model much depends on what is seen as 'minimal back-up service'. If this were interpreted as enabling people to participate fully in society, it would require a considerable improvement in the present level of provision that is made for, for example, people on supplementary benefit, and the standard of much publicly provided housing. If it were interpreted as meeting only basic physical and social needs the level of provision would be much less generous. The state's role in setting and enforcing minimum standards of practice and provision could be a considerable undertaking, as the difficulties in regulating the present mushrooming of homes for elderly people shows. Again the standard of what was acceptable in the private sector would be much influenced by what was provided by the state by way of 'minimal back-up service'. If the standard were low this would tend to depress the standard of what was offered at the bottom end of the market in the private sector and similarly if the standard in the state sector were high, the lowest standard in the private sector would also need to be high.

7.36   The model cannot be dismissed as automatically failing to meet the challenge of the concept of interdependence. It depends very much on the spirit in which such a model is implemented. If the intention were that no one should be prevented from playing their full role in society because of unemployment and disability one could argue that it met that challenge. However there are grounds for doubting whether this would be the case. The danger is that those who were unable to make provision for themselves by private and voluntary means, would receive second class treatment, and would be seen and would indeed perceive themselves as second class citizens. Services which are directed solely to the poor are almost invariably poor services. A major problem would be old age. Most private health schemes are not able to cope with the demands that are made by elderly people and exclude them from their schemes if they make claims on them over a certain limit. What sort of care would such elderly people receive under this system?

7.37   A serious risk is that this model could lead to a system of public welfare which would become a form of public charity to keep people from sinking below the breadline rather than a means for tackling the persistent reality of poverty and for ensuring that all can participate fully as citizens in society. The danger of the state involving itself only in the care of those who cannot care for themselves is that those people begin to be seen as failures, and that welfare provision then becomes a one-way relationship of giving by the better-off and receiving by the poor.

MODEL 3: THE STATE AS PRIMARY FUNDER

7.38   This model accepts the need to see that some services are provided for the whole community irrespective of their circumstances. It means that the state must, on behalf of all, play a leading role in financing services. Further, the state would play a role in setting standards and objectives for services. However, with this approach the actual provision of services is made by a variety of statutory, voluntary and private institutions. This might offer greater choice and flexibility.

7.39   This model has attractive features. It is strong on allowing flexible responses to changing needs and can offer people a real choice. The dilemmas concern how it would actually function in a deeply divided society. How is the universal availability of services to be guaranteed? How are the poor and weak to be protected from the capacity of wealthier and stronger people to gain the best out of the system through a more effective deployment of choice? How are standards of service to be guaranteed and maintained? How are the services to be co-ordinated? Will it lead to inefficient duplication and unhelpful competition between agencies? It is important for there to be some agreement about what should be expected of private and voluntary bodies and what should be the responsibility of public services. For example, many voluntary bodies are involved in the child care field and there is general acceptance of the important contribution they make, but privately run school examination systems would be a very different question. The diversity would give choice but could we be sure that it allowed choice for all between services of an acceptable standard?

MODEL 4: THE STATE AS PRIMARY PROVIDER

7.40   This model accepts and values the place of voluntary and private agencies but believes that comprehensive cover can only be guaranteed when public services are set up on a community-wide basis. In the course of this report we have identified some of the problems with this model which bears some resemblance to our present system, many of which stem from the use of large-scale organisations. These make it liable to be paternalistic, cumbersome, removed from those it is serving and poor at fostering a sense of interdependence. It could be argued that contributing to the common good through taxation is an expression of interdependence. In practice the taxation system is often experienced as an imposition, and often by those who at the same time benefit most from it.

7.41 The problems of this model are real enough. Large organisations tend to be strongly resistant to change. Although it would be wrong to assume that nothing can be done to make services under this model sensitive, participatory and responsive, attempts to bring large-scale health and welfare organisations closer to the needs of those who use them have shown how difficult the task is. The efforts of many women and men of goodwill and dedication have been thwarted, often by the sheer size of the organisations. This suggests that the extent of the changes that could be needed is perhaps more radical than is often acknowledged. It may mean a recognition that to attempt to reform the procedures of large organisations is to tackle the problem at the wrong level. It may mean that more fundamental questions about the relevance of size and structures of the organisations and the ways in which they are managed and to whom they are accountable need to be considered. In general, however, those who argue for this approach see the future as requiring the reform of what we in this country have inherited rather than a radical change of philosophy. It is an open question whether the reforms that are being considered are radical enough.

MODEL 5: THE STATE AS EXCLUSIVE PROVIDER

7.42 In this model all voluntary and private provision is excluded completely and all services are provided by the state. There is no doubt here about where responsibility lies and in theory it should be easier to organise a comprehensive integrated system. In practice the problems of large-scale organisation noted under Model 4 are likely to be even more severe and choice is severely restricted.

7.43 The main criticism of this model is that taken to its logical conclusion it is almost unworkable in practice. It depends on an all-embracing philosophy of the state and, in practice, a Marxist framework. It is not clear how the family fits in and a rigid exclusion of the caring capacity of relatives, friends and neighbours would be an intolerable limitation of human creativity and compassion. However benevolent the motives of those funding and providing such a comprehensive system of state services, history suggests that the end result is likely to be experienced as an impersonal and insensitive monopoly which cannot take account of individual needs and wishes. At root it is hard, if not impossible, for such a monolithic approach to welfare to be personal.

Where Do We Stand?

7.44   This report cannot give a definitive judgement on where Christians should stand in relation to these complex issues. We have to be mature enough to live with complexity and uncertainty. As we indicated in our description of Model 2, much depends on *how* these models are implemented. For example, Model 2, where the role of the state is restricted to that of a safety net, could be implemented in a generous spirit which was determined to see that poor people, elderly people, and people with disabilities were not treated as second-class citizens but were enabled to play a full part in society. If so those who are suspicious of the safety net model might then have fewer anxieties about it. Again Model 4, where the state is the main funder, could be implemented in the same generous spirit, with a determination to achieve a real flexibility and sensitivity to the needs and aspirations of those requiring services, and a realisation of the importance of enabling people to contribute as well as receive. This would make interdependence a reality, and the anxieties of those who fear the power of large organisations might be reduced.

7.45   But the way in which a model is implemented must not blind us to each model's inherent strengths and weaknesses. Decisions have to be taken about what the main direction of policy should be. The models, simplified though they are, do represent the main options.

7.46   We have tried to outline the basic theological assumptions with which Christians may approach these questions. Our conclusions owe much to the importance we attach to the notion of interdependence, and the love of God expressed as justice to the poor and the oppressed. Our understanding of the kingdom of God helps us to recognise the incomplete and partial response that we are bound to make to this great truth.

7.47 With these theological truths in mind, and given our particular history of welfare provision, it seems to this working group that Models 1 and 5 can be put on one side. Model 1 fails to acknowledge the central importance of interdependence and offers no real hope that the poor and disadvantaged would be accorded the dignity and standard of living which they are entitled to expect. Model 5 also fails in relation to interdependence. Although interdependence is reflected in the formal state structures of welfare, such a system is too rigid to encompass the range of ways in which a mutual interdependence on one another needs to be able to find expression. It does not take adequate account of the richness of human diversity and creativity. Model 2, 'the safety net', cannot be dismissed so easily, especially if all you want to do is to help the poor. However in practice there are considerable difficulties with implementing Model 2. There is the problem of how the poor are defined; indeed defining the poor as such is almost bound to lead to stigma and divisiveness. Despite the current move towards a system akin to Model 2, we do not feel that this model either reflects a true understanding of interdependence or is likely to give sufficient security to the most vulnerable members of society.

7.48 This brings us to Models 3 and 4. A firm framework of public welfare services seems to us essential. We believe that the best way of providing major services is through the development of services which can meet the basic needs of all citizens irrespective of their ability to pay. We are only likely to be able to meet the needs of the weak and vulnerable — which may include all of us at different points of our lives — if the services recognise their special needs and do not push them to the margins of society. In justifying this conclusion, we return once again to the basic truths which we believe must underlie any system of welfare. It must be concerned with the well-being of all members of society: the notion of interdependence and concern for the poor and oppressed demands no less. Any model which splits off the least fortunate members of society and treats them in a way which is fundamentally different from the rest is unacceptable. Any model which fails to give members of society the opportunity and means to express their mutual interdependence on one another and to give and receive from one another, is inadequate. Social integration, that elusive but vital sense of belonging together, therefore seems to us most likely to be achieved with Models 3 and 4.

7.49   Generous provision of services by society through the state is essential. But it is not enough on its own to produce the kind of society we wish to see. A mixed economy of welfare, built on co-operation between the public, voluntary and private sectors is to be welcomed.

7.50   We thus affirm much of the vision, if not the detail, of the post-war settlement, which was fundamentally sound. Nevertheless, there have been major and complex changes in our society since then, which this report has shown, and which require us to move on. These changes however have done nothing to undermine our belief that society has a duty to see that all its citizens are provided for, and that the public provision of a sound infrastructure of services is crucial to this end.

7.51   We are not arguing for the status quo. We have made it clear that there are weaknesses in the welfare state at the moment. The resurgence of mass unemployment, the use of large-scale means-testing, increasing poverty and growing inequality gives cause for grave anxiety. We have shown too that it is the better off who profit most from the welfare state rather than the most disadvantaged. This is unacceptable. We recognise that the charges of paternalism have much justification, that elements of greater participation are to be welcomed, that organisations need to be flexible and responsive, that new insights about the roles of men and women need to be recognised.

7.52   The welfare state will need to look different in the future, and will need to find ways of taking all these themes very seriously indeed. Difficult political choices will have to be made if the vision of the war-time years is to have any chance of being fulfilled in our own generation.

7.53   It will not be good enough just to try more of the same. We live in a fundamentally changed society and cannot ignore the realities of our economic climate. Whichever model or whichever combination of models we choose, it cannot be considered apart from how it will be implemented. It will have to relate to a predominantly post-industrial society in which unhealthy dependence is avoided and all can participate fully.

7.54   We have not thought it right to spell out the implications of these themes for particular policies. The report of the Archbishop's Commission on Urban Priority Areas, *Faith in the City*, makes a number of recommendations, which should receive serious consideraton. Every reader will need to reflect on the implications for the areas of life where he or she is most involved.

Conclusion

7.55   There are some developments today which Christians cannot approve. First, Christians cannot, it seems to us, accept an individualist philosophy which demands that the individual stand on his or her own feet come what may. Rather we should be trying to move towards a welfare society where we are ready to take some responsibility for each other's pain and each other's needs, to ask for help unashamedly, and also, within this framework of interdependence, to grow to maturity measured by nothing less than the full stature of Christ (Ephesians 4.13). As one response from Newcastle put it 'The Church must show that policies shot through with compassion are evidence of strength not weakness. That the weak as well as the strong, the regional as well as the central, must be involved in the patterns and processes that lead to policy formulation.'[5]

7.56   Second, Christians must be concerned about the divisions within our society, that polarisation which *Faith in the City* describes in detail.[6] We cannot approve a system which allows a large minority of our population to live at a level of income which sinks lower and lower in comparison with the wage-earning majority. The grim facts of gross inequality between the very (and sometimes excessively) rich and the poor is for us not just a social misfortune but a social evil. It is vital to try to reduce the divisions of wealth and opportunity rather than simply allow them to get sharper. This is hardly a new challenge. In 1911, when Cosmo Gordon Lang was Archbishop of Canterbury, he spoke to a London Men's Rally on this point: 'The nineteenth century was concerned with the creation of wealth. The twentieth century will be concerned with its distribution. We cannot but be appalled by the contrast of increasing prosperity and of great poverty. Our true self in the contemplation of this inequality says these things should not be.'[7] The challenge is still with us, but not, as Lang had anticipated, just as far as distribution was concerned but also with regard to the creation of wealth. *New Society*, in its comment on publication of *Social Trends* 1986, remarked that we appear to be pulling up the drawbridge to our homes;[8] standards of living in the homes of those who are employed are rising, while public services are allowed to become shabbier, and the lives of those in relative poverty to become ever more difficult.

7.57   Third, Christians must be wary of trends which divide the nation into those who draw on social security and those who do not. Our Christian understanding is that, not just within the Christian community but within society as a whole, 'we are members one of another'. In the light of this, welfare provision should not just be about directing benefits to the very poor. It should be concerned with justice for all citizens and any tendency to allow the development of a socially disenfranchised sub-class of those receiving benefit is unacceptable.

7.58   For Christians more is required in response to the injustice and pain experienced by those at the margins of society than just reasonableness. What is needed in response to deprivation and despair is passion, a passionate refusal to accept that homelessness, poor housing, inadequate education, unemployment, racism, poverty and the sadness and hopelessness that go with them are tolerable or inevitable. In this respect Christians should be persistent and refuse to accept that nothing can be done. There will be disagreements, undoubtedly, about how these issues should be tackled but it is not open to Christians to ignore them, as the parable of the sheep and the goats (Matthew 25) makes inescapably clear. It is up to Christians, along with all who have these concerns, to ensure that questions of social justice are placed firmly on the agenda of the political parties. How we as a society can respond adequately to the poor is a matter of active and urgent political debate. The divisions in our society between black and white, rich and poor, those in jobs and those without, deprived inner cities and prosperous suburbs, should be subject to careful and urgent analysis and ways sought of removing injustices.

7.59   That is easy to write and easy to read but how is it possible to create the sheer determination, the moral passion needed to tackle the deep-seated ills of our society? It is not obviously in the interests of comfortable Britain to understand the problems of uncomfortable Britain. It is far easier on the conscience to remain unaware of the acute deprivation to which many of our fellow citizens are subject. There is as much need for Christians and those who are like-minded and like-hearted to understand with their hearts as there is for them to understand with their minds. For Christians who worship the God who became incarnate and was subject to the hardships of life on this earth, and not a very privileged life at that, there would seem to be a particular responsibility for those who are more affluent to discover a little of what it is like to be poor and deprived. Christians have a special calling to build bridges of understanding, across the divisions of class, of wealth and poverty, of race, of gender, which divide and disfigure our society.

7.60   In particular it is first hand encounter between comfortable Britain and those at the receiving end of the painful consequences of our present social structures and social policies which will help to provide the moral passion that is needed to ensure that none of the political parties is allowed to dodge these fundamental issues.

7.61   A welfare state cannot be imposed or kept in being unless it is sustained and supported by a society which is genuinely concerned for the welfare and well-being of all its members. Christians as members of society have a responsibility to play their part in determining what values society holds dear. If the Church were to encourage the building of links and bridges across the barriers which divide our society, Christians would be in a better position to play that role effectively and ensure that ours was a society in which justice and compassion were valued, and the interdependence of one on another was acknowledged and accepted.

7.62   The introduction to this report told the stories of Maureen, newly discharged from mental handicap hospital; of Mr Smith looking after his frail mother; of Christine's death in a hospice; of Mr Taylor and his family, facing up to redundancy and possibly long-term unemployment; of Pauline and her family's fight to keep going in sub-standard housing. Their lives contained personal struggle, bleakness and suffering. But they also contained hope. People can and do care deeply for each other; the partnership of welfare services can free people to become more fully themselves.

7.63   It is right to return to these stories in these last pages and perhaps to call to mind ourselves some of the people whom we know and love who have needed a great deal of help. It is right to remember that suffering and hope are intimately connected, and that the debate about the welfare state is ultimately about the wellbeing of us all.

7.64   The welfare state in Britain faces difficulties, but it has achieved much. We have set out the current situation, the challenges and the debate and have provided important clues to the way forward. It is now for the Church and, we hope, the nation to consider this analysis and to develop policies to meet the demands of this vision.

REFERENCES

Chapter 1

1. *The Future of the Welfare State.* Social Policy Committee of the General Synod Board for Social Responsibility, 1984.

2. *Reform of Social Security.* Green Paper. Cmnds. 9517-9520. HMSO, 1985. *Reform of Social Security. Programme for Action.* Cmnd. 9691. HMSO, 1985.

3. *Primary Health Care: an Agenda for Discussion.* Cmnd. 9771. HMSO, 1986.

4. The Swann Report: *Education for All.* Cmnd. 9453. HMSO, 1985.

5. *The Report of the Inquiry into British Housing.* National Federation of Housing Associations, 1985.

6. *Faith in the City.* The Report of the Archbishop of Canterbury's Commission on Urban Priority Areas. Church House Publishing, 1985.

7. *Transnational Corporations.* CIO, 1983. *Let Justice Flow: A Contribution to the debate about development.* Church House Publishing, 1985.

8. Chester Board for Social Responsibility.

9. The benefit rates mentioned in this case study are 1985/86 rates.

Chapter 2

1. Race, D. Personal statement from the Children's Society.

2. Logan, P. Southwark Diocesan Single Homeless Group.

3. Birmingham Diocesan Social Responsibility Council.

4. Chester Board for Social Responsibility.

5. Nozick, R. *Anarchy, State and Utopia.* Blackwell, 1974.
   Hayek, F.A. *The Constitution of Liberty.* Routledge and Kegan Paul, 1960.

6. Niebuhr, R. *Moral Man and Immoral Society.* Scribners, 1932.

Chapter 3

1. Table 1.1. Age and Sex Structure of the Population. *Social Trends.* HMSO, 1986.

2. Table 7.1. Expectations of Life from Birth and from Specific Ages. *Social Trends.* HMSO, 1986.

3. Table 1.1. *Social Trends.* Op. cit.

4. Berthoud, R. (ed.) *Challenges to Social Policy.* Gower, 1985.

5. Titmuss, R.M. *Essays on the Welfare State.* George Allen and Unwin, 1963.

6. Study Commission on the Family. *Values and the Changing Family.* A Final report from the Working Party on Values. Whitley Press Ltd., 1982.

7. Ibid.

8. Walker, A. *The Care Gap: How Can Local Authorities meet the needs of the Elderly?* Local Government Information Unit, 1985.

9. Parker, G. *With Due Care and Attention; a Review of Research on Informal Care.* Family Policy Studies Centre, 1985.

10. Equal Opportunities Commission. *Caring for the Elderly and Handicapped: Community Care Policies and Women's Lives.* EOC, 1982.

11. Martin, J. and Roberts, C. *Women and Employment: a Lifetime Perspective.* Department of Employment/Office of Population Censuses and Surveys. HMSO, 1984.

12. *The Family Today.* Family Policy Studies Centre, 1986.

13. Ibid.

14. Table 2.15. Divorce. *Social Trends.* HMSO, 1986.

15. Haskey, J. The Proportion of Marriages Ending in Divorce. *Population Trends 27.* HMSO, 1982.

16. Haskey, J. Marital Status Before Marriage and Age at Marriage: Their Influence on the Chance of Divorce. *Population Trends 32.* HMSO, 1983.

17. *One-Parent Families.* Family Policy Studies Centre, 1984. (Projected estimate from 1981 census figures by the National Council for One-Parent Families.)

18. Based on Local Authority Analysis Tables 34,38. *Census 1981 England and Wales.* Vol. 17. Greater London. This figure refers to households containing at least one one-parent-family with dependent children under 25.

19. Estimates from the Family Expenditure Survey. HMSO, 1985. Quoted by the National Council of One-Parent Families.

20. Table 1.15. Migrant Flows: By Age and Citizenship. *Social Trends.* HMSO, 1986.

21. Brown, C. *Black and White Britain.* Policy Studies Institute. Heinemann, 1984.

22. See, for example, Smith D. *The Facts of Racial Disadvantage: a National Survey.* PEP, 1976.

23. See, for example, *Race and Council Housing in Hackney: Report of a Formal Investigation.* CRE, 1984.
Race and Housing in Liverpool: a Research Report. CRE, 1984.

24. *Racial Discrimination.* Cmnd. 6234. HMSO, 1975.

25. Connelly, N. *Social Services Departments and Race: A Discussion Paper.* Policy Studies Institute, 1985.
Young, K. and Connelly, N. *Policy and Justice in the Multi-Racial City.* Policy Studies Institute, 1981.

26. Manpower Services Commission *Annual Report* HMSO, 1985.

27. Martin, J. and Roberts, C. Op. cit.

28. *And All that is Unseen: Women and Work.* Church House Publishing, 1986.

29. *Social Security Statistics.* HMSO, 1983.

30. Beveridge, W. *The Pillars of Security.* George Allen and Unwin, 1943.

31. *Social Security Statistics.* Op. cit.

32. Ibid.

33. *Poverty Paper No. 52.* Child Poverty Action Group, 1982.

34. *Caring for Unemployed People.* Report by the Association of Metropolitan Authorities. Bedford Square Press, 1985.
Hunt S. *Health and Social Deprivation in Camberwell Health District.* King's College School of Medicine, Unpublished, 1986.

35. Table 4.24. Unemployment Rates: By Region. *Social Trends.* HMSO, 1986.

36. OPCS Local Authority Vital Statistics 1981. Series VS No. 8. Table 1.

37. *Faith in the City.* Op. cit.

Chapter 4

1. Rowntree, B.S. *Poverty and Progress : A Second Social Survey of York.* Longman, 1941.

2. Ministry of Pensions. *Annual Report.* HMSO, 1950.

3. Dilnot, A.W., Kay, J.A., and Morris, C.N. *The Reform of Social Security.* Clarendon Press, 1984.

4. Bean, P. et al. *In Defence of Welfare.* Tavistock Publications, 1985.

5. House of Commons *Hansard.* 2 February, 1983. Vol. 36. Col. 128.

6. Chart 5.16. Net weekly spending power: By gross earnings and type of family, April 1985. *Social Trends.* HMSO, 1986.

7. Donnison, D. *The Politics of Poverty.* Martin Robertson, 1982.

8. *Social Security Statistics.* HMSO, 1983.

9. Ibid.

10. Ibid.

11. Cooper, S. *The Health Benefits (Family Income Supplement Part 5).* Policy Studies Institute, 1985.

12. *Report of the Inquiry into British Housing.* National Federation of Housing Associations, 1985.

13. House of Commons *Hansard.* 9 April 1986. Vol. 95. Col. 125.

14. Table 8.19. Renovations: By Tenure. *Social Trends.* HMSO, 1986.

15. *Election Briefing.* Shelter, 1983.

16. Table 6.23. Public Expenditure in Real Terms: By Programme. *Social Trends.* HMSO, 1986.

17. *Roof,* July/August 1986. Shelter, 1986.

18. Table 8.21. Homeless Households accepted by local authorities: by priority need category. *Social Trends.* HMSO, 1986.

19. *Report of the Committee on Local Authority and Allied Personal Social Services.* (The Seebohm Report.) Cmnd. 3703. HMSO, 1968.

20. See, for example, the Report of the Select Committee for Social Services. *Children in Care.* HMSO, 1984.

21. *Social Workers: their Role and Tasks* (The Barclay Report). Bedford Square Press, 1982.

22. Berthoud, R., Brown, J.C., and Cooper, S. *Poverty and the Development of Anti-Poverty Policies in the U.K.* Policy Studies Institute, 1981.

23. Department of Education and Science Statistics, 1985.

24. Berthoud, R. et al. Op. Cit.

25. Pilkington, A. *Race Relations in Britain.* University Tutorial Press, 1984.

26. The Swann Report *Education for All.* Cmnd. 9453. HMSO, 1985.

27. Halsey, A. H. *Origins and Destinations—Family, Class and Education in Modern Britain.* Clarendon Press, 1980.

28. Report of Her Majesty's Inspectors on the Effects of Local Authorities Expenditure Policies on Education Provision in England 1985.

Chapter 5

1. Monmouth Diocesan Council for Social Responsibility.

2. The Black Report. *Inequalities in Health.* DHSS, 1980.

3. Newbigin, L. *The Welfare State. A Christian Perspective.* Oxford Institute for Church and Society, 1985.

4. Chelmsford Diocese Board of Mission

5. Billings A., Sheffield

6. London Diocesan Board for Social Responsibility

7. See, for example, Jowell, R. and Witherspoon, S. *British Social Attitudes: the 1985 report.* Gower, 1985.

8. Bennett, F. 'The State, Welfare and Women's Dependence' in Segal, L. (ed.) *What is to be done about the Family?* Penguin, 1983.

9. Finch, J. and Groves, D. (eds.) *A Labour of Love: Women, Work and Caring.* Routledge and Kegan Paul, 1983.

10. DHSS Personal Social Services *Local Authority Statistics.* HMSO, 1976.

11. *General Household Survey.* HMSO, 1981.

12. *Better Services for the Mentally Ill.* HMSO, 1975.

13. *Inpatient Statistics for the Mental Health Enquiry for England 75.19.* Statistics and Research Report Series 20. HMSO, 1977.

14. Wilson, E. 'Feminism and Social Policy' in Loney, M., Boswell D. and Clarke, J. (eds.) *Social Policy and Social Welfare.* Open University Press, 1983.

15. Segal, L. Op. cit.

16. See, for example, Wilson, A. *Finding a Voice: Asian Women in Britain.* Virago, 1978.
Campbell, B. *Wigan Pier Revisited.* Virago, 1984.
Oliver, J. and Briggs, A. *The Experience of Caring.* Routledge and Kegan Paul, 1985.

17. Segal, L. Op. cit.

18. Friedman, M. *Capitalism and Freedom.* University of Chicago Press, 1962.
Friedman, M. and Friedman, R. *Free to Choose.* Secker and Warburg, 1980.

19. Hayek. F.A. *The Constitution of Liberty.* Routledge and Kegan Paul, 1960.

20. Nozick, R. *Anarchy, State and Utopia.* Blackwell, 1974.

21. Illich, I. *Deschooling Society.* Penguin, 1973.

22. Illich, I. *Limits to Medicine.* Boyars, 1976.

23. Hadley, R. and Hatch, S. *Social Welfare and the Failure of the State.* George Allen and Unwin, 1981.

Chapter 6

1. Tables 3.2 and 7.48. *Social Trends.* HMSO, 1986.

2. Glennerster, H. *Paying for Welfare.* Blackwell, 1985.

3. Chart 3.14.6 Health and Personal Social Services. Gross Current Expenditure per head by age group 1983-1984. *The Government's Expenditure Plans 1986-1987 to 1988-1989.* Cmnd. 9702-II. HMSO, 1986.

4. Glennerster, H. Op. cit.

5. Davis, E. and Kay, J. 'Expanding the VAT base' in *Fiscal Studies*. Vol. 6. No.1. February, 1985. Institute of Fiscal Studies, 1985.

6. King, M. and Fullerton, D. *Taxation of Income from Capital: A Comparative Study of the United States, the United Kingdom, Sweden and West Germany*. University of Chicago Press, 1984.

7. Le Grand, J. *The Strategy of Equality*. George Allen and Unwin, 1982.

8. Taylor Gooby and Papadakis E. 'Who Wants the Welfare State?' in *New Society*. 19th July, 1975.

Chapter 7

1. Larkin, P. *High Windows*. Faber, 1974.

2. Chart 39. Private Medical Insurance. *Social Trends*. HMSO, 1986.

3. London Diocesan Board for Social Responsibility.

4. House of Commons *Hansard* 12 June 1984. Vol. 61. Col. 460.

5. Smith G., Newcastle.

6. *Faith in the City*. Op. cit.

7. Lockhart, J.G. *Cosmo Gordon Lang*. Hodder & Stoughton, 1949.

8. *New Society*. 10 January 1986.

FURTHER READING

Anderson, D., Lait, J and Marsland, D. *Breaking the Spell of the Welfare State.* Social Affairs Unit, 1981.

Atherton, J. *The Scandal of Poverty.* Mowbrays, 1983.

Berthoud, R. (ed.) *Challenges to Social Policy.* Gower, 1985.

Faith in the City A call for action by church and nation. The report of the Archbishop of Canterbury's Commission on Urban Priority Areas. Church House Publishing, 1985.

Forrester, D. *Christianity and the Future of Welfare.* Epworth, 1985.

Friedman, M and Friedman, R. *Free to Choose.* Penguin, 1980.

George V., and Wilding P. *Ideology and Social Welfare.* Routledge and Kegan Paul, 1985.

Klein, R. and O'Higgins, M. *The Future of Welfare.* Blackwell, 1985.

Leech, K. *The Social God.* Sheldon Press, 1981.

Mishra, R. *The Welfare State in Crisis.* Wheatsheaf, 1985.

Newbigin, L. *The Other Side of 1984.* World Council of Churches, 1983.

Orchard, S. *A Christian Appreciation of the Welfare State.* British Council of Churches, 1985.

Preston, R.H. *Religion and the Rise of Capitalism.* SCM Press, 1979.

Reform of Social Security. Cmnd. 9517. HMSO. 1985.

Tawney, R.H. *Equality.* Allen and Unwin, 1964.

Temple, W. *Christianity and the Social Order.* Penguin, 1942.

Titmuss, R.M. *Essays on the Welfare State.* Allen and Unwin, 1963.

Sheppard, D. *Bias to the Poor.* Hodder, 1983.

Terrill, R. *R.H. Tawney and His Times.* Deutsch, 1973.

Walter, T. *Fair Shares.* An ethical guide to tax and social security. Handsel Press (Edinburgh), 1985.

LIST OF RESPONDENTS

1. Fran Bennett, Child Poverty Action Group
2. Rev. Alan Billings
3. Birmingham Council for Social Responsibility
4. Chelmsford Diocese Board of Mission
5. Chester Board for Social Responsibility
6. *Christian Statesman*
7. Elizabeth Dodds, Liverpool Diocese
8. Captain Terry Drummond, Church Army
9. Ely Diocesan Board for Social Responsibility
10. Tom Gilbert, Norwich Board for Social Responsibility
11. Rt Hon. J.S. Gummer, MP
12. Dr Robert Holman, Children's Society
13. Hospital Chaplaincies Council
14. Leicester Board for Social Responsibility
15. Lichfield Board for Social Responsibility
16. Dr Pat Logan
17. London Diocesan Board for Social Responsibility
18. Manchester Board for Social Responsibility
19. Monmouth Council for Social Responsibility
20. The Mothers' Union
21. Rev. C.J. Moody, Cambridgeshire Area Health Authority
22. Dr P.E. Nixon
23. Peterborough Diocese Group for Social Responsibility
24. Church of England Diocesan Social Workers
25. David Race, Children's Society
26. Rev. Canon Geoffrey Smith, Newcastle Diocese
27. Southwark Diocesan Board for Mission and Social Responsibility
28. Southwell Diocese
29. Morlais Thomas, Children's Society
30. Rev. Malcolm Torry, South London Industrial Mission
31. Sir William Van Straubenzee, MP
32. Professor Paul Wilding, University of Manchester
33. Rev. Paul Wilson, Southern Derbyshire Area Health Authority
34. Winchester Council for Social Responsibility
35. John Hughes, Ruskin College, Oxford